Old Houses in Rockingham County Revisited
1750-1850

Ann Terrell Baker

Peak Publishing
Harrisonburg, Virginia

Cover and interior design by Mayapriya Long
Bookwrights Design
www.bookwrights.com

Cover photo of Smithland (*see page 147 for story*) by Polly Frye

Printed in the United States of America

Published by
Peak Publishing
541 Myers Avenue
Harrisonburg, Virginia 22801
webake@cfw.com

Library of Congress Catalog Card Number: 99-62548
International Standard Book Number: 0-9671765-0-6

This book is dedicated to someone who
taught me to love the past, the
present and the future.
Cheers, Dad

Ann Jerrell Baker

CONTENTS

FOREWORD

Every house has a story. My father realized this when he wrote the first edition of *Old Houses in Rockingham County, 1750-1850*, in 1967. I helped with the photography and anything else he could talk me into doing for this project. So, when my husband and I returned to Harrisonburg after a twenty five year absence, one of the first tasks I did was to check on some of the homes that were in my father's book. Only a few were in poor condition. The rest had either undergone remarkable transformations or were still beautiful. I got hooked. When I searched out some of these homeowners, I found that much more information was available now and the old photos that I saw were wonderful. It was difficult to ignore the importance of these homes and their connection to the rich history of Rockingham County.

This book is the result of a two year effort of interviews and collecting information. None of this would have been possible without the total support and cooperation of the homeowners. Most of them had remembered my dad and the first book. They soon became interested in this project also. Many doors were open because my father was an active local historian and a gentleman.

This book contains exactly the same houses he researched. Initially, I had an idea to include many more homes. But, I was quickly overwhelmed and decided that is another project entirely. Also, I decided to eliminate the barns and dependencies that were in the original version. Most of the barns are gone now and I wanted to emphasize the main house. Dependencies are mentioned only to complete the mental picture of the layout of the house on the property. The names of the homeowners and the locations of these home are purposely omitted to protect their privacy. It was a controversial decision but, after much thought, I felt that the purpose of this book is historical not for tour groups. Any individual that has a special interest in any house can contact the Harrisonburg-Rockingham Historical Society. The houses that are registered with the Virginia Landmarks Registry and/or the National Registry of Historic Places are noted at the bottom of each text with the initials of the registries. (VLR or NRHP)

Help came from many sources and my thanks go to many people. My husband is not a native of the area and he found himself quickly immersed in history and on roads he did not even know existed. He was the main photographer and a companion on many trips out to the county. We often made an event out of these trips by taking friends and a picnic with us.

Special thanks to Darryl Nash who gave much needed editing and history lessons. Other editors are to be thanked as the text seemed to be constantly changing. The Harrisonburg-Rockingham County Historical Society and Fort Harrison, Inc. provided support and information. Ruth Greenwald at Bridgewater College, Bridgewater, Virginia and Rebecca Ebert at Handley Library, Winchester, Virginia helped me sort though the volumes of information from John Wayland. Elizabeth Gushee at the Library of Virginia and Bryan Green at the Virginia Historical Society helped me locate some valuable photographs. Casey Billhimer of the Elkton Historical Society and Miss Kite helped me with the history of the Elkton area.

Professional photographer Polly Frye photographed the cover house and was invaluable in critiquing the candid photographs that we took on our own. All the supplemental photos, unless otherwise noted, were provided by the homeowners. Thanks to the homeowners of Smithland for allowing me to place their home on the cover. It was my great grandparents' home and I thought it would be a nice tribute to them.

There are two purposes of this book. One is to show the history of Rockingham County through the lives of the homeowners, both present and past. Secondly, it serves to record the current state of the homes that were in the original book thirty years ago. I hope you enjoy reading about the personalities and history that made up this time period in Rockingham County. Every house does have a story.

Old Houses in Rockingham County Revisited

INTRODUCTION

On a topographical map, the Commonwealth of Virginia is made up of three different provinces. On the east coast, there is the Tidewater area that is low, flat and sandy country. Further west into a higher elevation, there is the Piedmont area which is more hilly with small valleys and wooded areas. In the western mountain section, known as Appalachia, there are two mountain ranges of the Blue Ridge and the Allegheny. Between these two mountain ranges lies the Shenandoah Valley.

Before 1738, Orange County contained the entire Shenandoah Valley, In 1738, Frederick and Augusta Counties were cut away from Orange County. Rockingham County was formed in 1778 from the northern part of Augusta County. The original county included part of the present counties of Page and Pendleton, now West Virginia. Rockingham is named for Lord Rockingham, an English peer who supported the colonies in the Stamp Act. The first meeting of the county court was held at the house of Daniel Smith near the settlement called "Rocktown", now Harrisonburg. Established in 1780, Harrisonburg was founded on land donated by Thomas Harrison and became the county seat.

The colony of Virginia was established in 1606, in the Tidewater section of the state. Here, there was prosperity and political activity. Cities flourished and there was a very sophisticated plantation life. However, at the same time, the land west of the Blue Ridge Mountains remained in almost complete isolation, despite efforts of the English governors of the state to encourage settlement and exploration into the Valley.

In 1716, Governor Spotswood made an expedition to the Valley. The purpose of this trip was to encourage settlement of the area. The trip was successful and word spread about the abundant land available. One of the first settlers was a Swiss, Jacob Stover, who received patents for lands in both Page and Rockingham Counties in 1730. Stover was unsuccessful in settling the Rockingham grant, and died in 1741. However, in 1739, Jost Hite and Robert McKay and their partners, William Duff and Robert Green, received a grant for 7009 acres in the Linville Valley in the present Rockingham County. Mostly Scots and Germans came into this region. But, in spite of the large number of Germans, the new county court fell under the control of the English speaking population. Of the thirteen men elected to the first county court, six were Scotch or Irish, three were English, two were Welsh, and two were German.

Part of the development of Rockingham County occurred as settlers from Shenandoah and other counties to the north followed a main wagon road south to the fertile drains of the North Fork of the Shenandoah River. Meanwhile, Swiss and German settlers came from the Piedmont through gaps, such as Swift Run Gap, east of Elkton, into the Rockingham County. Another route for settlers into Rockingham was by way of Brocks Gap into Linville Valley, Such migrations occurred during the French and Indian War as settlers were forced to flee their homes in the Alleghenies and seek refuge in the Valley. Later migration was made directly from Pennsylvania through the Valley of the Potomac and through the passes in the mountains.

One of the most significant factors leading to the settlement of Rockingham was the Fairfax line. In 1745, the line was laid down and it passed about two miles south of New Market, Shenandoah County. Settlers could locate south of the line in Rockingham and avoid the rents to Lord Fairfax. Here, they paid taxes directly to the government of Virginia. With the initiation of the Fairfax line, titles to many tracts of land in Shenandoah and Frederick Counties were in doubt, making the purchase of land in Rockingham even more appealing.

Unlike the first settlers in Virginia who arrived unequipped to build shelter, the settlers to this area had already been established in this new world. Many of these homes are duplicates of what existed in their native lands. The first settlement was in the eastern portion of the county, east of Massanutten Mountain. These people were of German and Swiss descent. But, at the same time, there is evidence that some settlement into the western part of the county was being done as early as 1734. These people located beyond the various creeks, like Linville Creek and Smith Creek. These people were mostly German, Scotch Irish and Swiss. These people were small farmers and were of religious orders such as Mennonite, Dunkard and Lutheran. They were conservative in their ideas as well as their life. Of this group of immigrants, the Scotch Irish and English moved further south and settled into the Augusta County area.

There were three basic styles of architecture.

PIONEER STYLE

This term is only for description purposes and it is not an "official" architectural term. It is used in this book to describe a style that was popular among early houses built by settlers of Rockingham County. Two examples of pioneer style houses found in this book are the Baxter House and the Martz-Harrison. It is patterned after what is known as the "salt box" style found in New England. Log houses were used very little in colonial America. The use of this material was not indigenous to the European countries from which these settlers originated. The idea of the log house was brought to the colonies by the Swedish and Finnish people who settled in Delaware in 1638. It was the Scotch-Irish who grasped the idea of the log house as a form of quick and inexpensive construction.

The pioneer house consisted of one large room, one and one half stories high. It had a cellar and a one storied addition to the rear. There was one chimney serving the main portion of the house, which was either at the end or the center of the house. There was also another fireplace serving the addition.

The large room was a multi purpose room being used for cooking, eating and sleeping. The half story, or loft, was used for storage or sleeping. The lean to extension to the rear was used for storage or for food preparation if there was a fireplace.

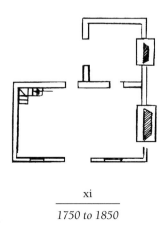

1750 to 1850

German Style

This house of the early German settlers can be distinguished from the houses of the English or non-German by the presence of a central chimney. The center chimney house was built in the county during the eighteenth century and was constructed either of stone or logs. There is no evidence of any having been built after 1800.

These houses were very basic in plan and typical of the German concern for function and little wasted space. The method of construction was simple. Four walls were constructed with two doors, one on the back and one on the front with windows on all four sides. The shape of the chimney in the center depended on the number of fireplaces it served. There could have been as many as six but usually it was four fireplaces. It was constructed of stone which ingenuously made it serve as a heating device as the stones, once warm, radiated heat throughout the house.

The interior space was divided off into rooms by vertical pine boards held in place by tongue and groove. These walls divided the house in half, centering on the chimney, which provided two rooms each with a fireplace.

A portion of one room was partitioned off as a hallway and from this hallway ascended a small circular staircase which led to the second floor. The staircases were unique, skillfully constructed and varied in width.

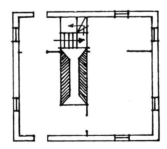

Old Houses in Rockingham County Revisited

ENGLISH STYLE

There also were the non-German or English style houses built in Rockingham County. This style is identified by the placing of two chimneys at either end and the use of a central hallway. The English style house was built in the county during the eighteenth and nineteenth centuries, although it was more common during the nineteenth century.

The English style house has a more rectangular shape and was built either in a story and a half or a full two stories with attic and basement. Floor plans follow any of the following arrangements.

1. Two on two

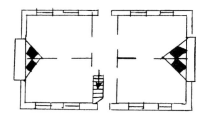

2. Three on three

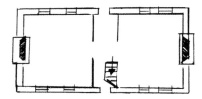

3. Four on four

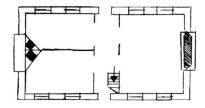

The house is divided by a center hallway which ran the depth of the structure with outside openings on both front and rear. From this hallway were doors opening into the rooms on the floor. To the rear of this hallway was an open staircase leading to the second floor. The second floor mirrored the first floor arrangement. In many houses, the staircase continued up into the attic.

The English house was built of stone, wood or brick. The use of brick in the county became very prevalent in the early nineteenth century and the majority of houses built between 1800 and 1850 were of this material. Clay found in the colonies was usable for making bricks and it was more economical to make them here rather than import them from England. Brick was not used in the seventeenth and eighteenth century because of the lack of lime for mortar. Bricks were usually made at the construction site. If the house was made of brick or stone, the chimneys were usually inside. On most of the frame structures, there were outside chimneys.

ॐ ॐ ॐ

This book deals only with selected houses in the 1750-1850 time frame. My father did add a few later ones in later updated editions of the book and those "newer" homes will be included in this edition. We begin this book, as he did, with one of the oldest house in Rockingham County built by Adam Miller. He personifies one of the patterns of settlement that was seen during this time period. Adam Miller was probably born around 1700 in Schreisheim, Germany. He came to Lancaster Pennsylvania with his wife. On a trip to Williamsburg, he heard of the beautiful Valley from one of the knights of Governor Spotswood and he followed their path across the Blue Ridge mountains with his family. His land came from the original patent that Jacob Stover owned. He lived on this property until he died in 1780.

Old Houses in Rockingham County Revisited

ADAM MILLER HOUSE
1727

Adam Miller was born in 1703, the son of Johann Peter and Ann Margaretha Miller. He left his home in Schreisheim, Germany, in the summer of 1720, along with his wife Barbara and sister Catrina, landing at Philadelphia and settling in the community of Germantown, in Lancaster County, Pennsylvania.

In 1716, Governor Spotswood left Williamsburg on August 20 for a trip across the Blue Ridge mountains. He returned to Williamsburg on September 17. The purpose of this trip was to encourage settlement of the western part of Virginia. (see River Bend) When Adam Miller visited Williamsburg, he heard from some of Spotswood's Knights of the Golden Horseshoe of the beautiful valley between the mountains. He moved up into the valley and began staking out a section of what is now referred to as the Upper Massanutten Lots, near the present Page County line. He later moved farther south and purchased 820 acres on the Shenandoah River near the present town of Elkton.

Adam Miller built this house of huge logs. Weather boarding now covers the logs. The interior walls are covered with plaster. It is a relatively small house, having two rooms on the first floor and two on the second. There is a central chimney with two fireplaces on the first floor. An enclosed staircase goes to the second floor.[1] Originally there were only two windows on the first floor one on either side. A window was later cut into the front of the house.

This house remained in the Miller family until 1936 when Miss Elizabeth Miller died. She was Adam Miller's great, great granddaughter and his last direct descendant. She willed the property to the University of Virginia Hospital. It was sold at public auction. The family that bought it stills retains ownership.

---

[1] United States Government, Works Progress Administration, "Historical American Buildings Survey, Rockingham County, 1935-1939," Bridgewater College, microfilm

Old Houses in Rockingham County Revisited

ADAM RADER HOUSE
1744

Many of the early German speaking settlers of Rockingham County brought with them not only their language but their various religious faiths: Mennonite, Dunkard, German Reform, Lutheran. Members of the Lutheran faith moved into the county around 1747, settled and established their churches. The German language was used by these people until 1838. It continued to be used in their church services as late as 1855.

Among these was the family of Adam Rader, who with eight children, had moved down from Lehigh County, Pennsylvania. Moravian missionaries, moving through the area in 1748, mention stopping at the plantation of a German named Adam Rader. Records show that Adam Rader had first leased 400 acres on March 14, 1744. The original patent was to Charles Robinson. After Adam Radar purchased this property, the deed mentions existing houses, barns, orchards, gardens, woodlands, etc. Whether Mr. Robinson or Mr. Radar built the present house cannot be determined.

The site was well chosen, facing onto Fort Run with water supplied by a large spring located west of the present town of Timberville. While there is no evidence of it having been built for defense purposes, the name of the stream could indicate that there might have been a fort in this area. Many of the larger, well built houses were designated as forts. Land grants of this period often required a "fort" structure to be built which served as the main house. Stockades and warning bells may have been added also to meet the requirements of the grant.

The house was built of logs, chinked with limestone, mortar and probably later weatherboarded. It was built into a bank so that it appeared to be a three story house. It was well proportioned and well built with two limestone end chimneys. The basement was only half excavated and had one room, which was used as a root cellar. The first floor was divided into three rooms. The east side was divided into two rooms with corner fireplaces, while the west side was one large room with fireplace and enclosed staircase. All walls were plastered and had chair rails. The mantels were hand carved. The west room fireplace wall was beautifully paneled presenting an extreme contrast in artistic endeavor to the exterior. The second floor was divided differently than the first. There was one large room on the south side extending the width of the house. The north side was divided into a small hallway and two small rooms.

On May 20, 1765, Adam Rader deeded three acres of land for the present Rader's Lutheran Church.[1] This deed included the statement that the land already included a meeting house as well as a school house and a burying ground. Adam Rader died April 18, 1773 and was buried in the family cemetery on the hill which overlooked his home. In his will he specified that his son, Adam, would inherit his plantation upon the death of his wife Barbara Anna. Of the remaining four sons and three daughters very little is known, except for Anthony Rader who became prominent in county affairs during the later part of the eighteenth century. He was elected one of the first justices in the courts of Rockingham County and was a captain in the militia from 1777 to 1779.

When this house was photographed in 1968, it was in a serious state of deterioration. Fortunately, this record exists as this house no longer stands.

---

[1] Henkel and Company's Lutheran Publication, New Market, VA, 1921, p6.

Daniel Harrison House
Fort Harrison
1749

Isaiah Harrison came to America about 1688 from Kingston Upon Hull, England. He first settled on Long Island, New York. Four sons and two daughters made the trip to Virginia. They settled first in Page County and later moved, in 1743, to what is now Rockingham County.

One of the sons, John, settled on Lacy Spring. Thomas built a stone house in Harrisonburg and Samuel settled on Linville Creek. Of the two sisters, Mary Harrison married Captain Robert Cravens who accompanied her to Virginia. Abigail Harrrison married Alexander Herron (Herring) who also accompanied her to Virginia. Their daughter, Bathsheba, married Abraham Lincoln and was the grandmother of President Abraham Lincoln.

The eldest son was Daniel Harrison who was a Captain in the Augusta County Militia. He was also a prosperous businessman. He had seven children with Margaret Cravens. After her death, he married Sarah Stephenson. His daughter Jane (Jean) married Daniel Smith, the owner of Smithland, a large house north of Harrisonburg. When Daniel Harrison died, he owned over a thousand acres. His plantation was inherited by his son Benjamin. This house remained in the Harrison family until 1821.

Daniel Harrison built this stone house as a protection against bands of Indians that roamed the Valley in the 1750's. The stone portion is the original part of the house. It was a two over two plan. On the first floor there was a corner staircase in the hall that ascended to the attic. There is now a central hall with an open staircase ascending to the second floor. There is no cellar in this house. Instead chestnut logs supported the ground floor and lay in the dirt.

This house has seen many changes over the years. It was first remodeled around 1856. A two story addition in the form of a brick ell made an extension to the north. This added four rooms with a two over two plan. There are two chimneys at the end of this wing serving two fireplaces on each floor. The original rear door served as one of the connections between the old and new sections. A window was enlarged to make another doorway. Additional changes were made in the 1860's. New windows were installed and interior changes were made. A new porch was added, and a stucco finish was placed over the stone exterior.

This property was purchased by Fort Harrison, Inc., in 1978. Because this house had been uninhabited for many years, a major restoration project was begun. The east and west walls were dismantled and rebuilt. Doors and windows were reset. The roof was replaced with one copied from the original roof. Inside all the woodwork was refinished. Walls and ceilings were replastered. It is furnished. Work was complete with the reconstruction of the summer kitchen behind the house in 1999.

Fort Harrison, Inc. operates the house as a museum.

1932 photograph taken by John Wayland; courtesy Handley Library, Winchester, Virginia.

1967 photograph taken by Isaac L. Terrell.

1750 to 1850

CRANEY ISLAND
1750

Andrew Byrd built this home. He was the son of Captain Andrew Byrd who was one of the early pioneer settlers in this area. On this property, the younger Andrew Byrd built mills and iron foundries. The Franklin Stoves which were made here were used throughout this section of the country. [1] His mills ground grain and were later known as the Craney Island Mills.

Andrew Byrd received a patent for the lands in 1749, and it is probable that he built his house shortly thereafter. It is a simple stated weatherboarded log house which sits on a slight rise above the creek. It was built in sections, the old portion being the north end. To the

---

[1] Good, William A, *Shadowed by the Massanutten*, printed by Commercial Press, Inc., Stephens City, Virginia, 1992, p. 236.

Old Houses in Rockingham County Revisited

back was a lean-to addition of stone which has been restored.[2]

This house has two stories with two end chimneys. There are six rooms, each with a fireplace. The mantels are plain. Some rooms have wainscoting and chair rails. Some of the original doors have handmade thumb latches remaining. The windows are original. The first floor windows have six over nine panes, while those on the second floor have six over six panes. The house is fronted with a four square column portico. The front door opens into a center hallway with an open staircase and a door opens to the rear of the house.[3]

This house was purchased by the current owners in 1966 at which time it was renovated.

Photograph of Craney Island taken by the Historic American Buildings Survey 1932; courtesy of the Library of Virginia, Richmond, Virginia.

---

[2] Interview with the homeowner.

[3] United States Government, Works Progress Administration, "Historical American Buildings Survey, Rockingham County, 1935-1939," Bridgewater College microfilm.

THOMAS HARRISON HOUSE
c.1750

This was the first house built in Harrisonburg. It was the home of Thomas Harrison, the founder of Harrisonburg. Thomas Harrison arrived, along with his father and brothers, from New York State in 1737. In 1744, he had acquired the land which he later developed as Harrisonburg. This house was the main house that stood on 1290 acres of land.

The courts of Rockingham County were held at Smithland for a season. Then, they were held at the Thomas Harrison House for some months while the first court house was being built. Thomas Harrison, and his second wife, Sarah, gave two and one half acres across the spring for public buildings. Courts, composed of county magistrates held monthly or bimonthly meetings in this house. Thomas Harrison was paid 100 pounds for five courts while Colonel Daniel Smith was paid 30 pounds for sixteen sessions. (see Smithland) Paper currency of the Revolutionary War was deteriorating.[1]

Many of the early Harrisons, including Thomas, were Methodists. It is felt that the early Methodist congregation met at this home. Tradition says that Bishop Francis Asbury was a frequent visitor in Harrisonburg, founded a school in the town in 1794 and also conducted the first conference of the Methodist Church held west of the Blue Ridge Mountains that same year. Around 1900 General John E. Roller used this house as his law offices. (see Inglewood)

It is a three story house of rubble limestone that originally faced east. Two exterior doors were located on this side, where a covered porch existed. An exterior stairway leads to the third floor.

The first floor, which is now partially underground, is entered from the rear or north side by way of a series of steps. It contains one large room with large fireplace and stone paved floor. This room was the kitchen. The two small, slotted windows here are probably for ventilation and protection of the food from theft.

The second floor was divided by tongue and groove pine board walls, each with corner fireplaces. Only one fireplace can be seen now; the other has been enclosed. Each room has an outside door and two windows. The rooms had attractive mantels and chair rails which were painted. The walls were plastered.

The third floor is one large room with two dormer windows, used for storage or sleeping. Moravians passing through the Valley in 1753 mentioned stopping at the home of Thomas Harrison. [2] It is possible that, while he did not operate an inn, this house was the place of shelter and hospitality for many early travelers.

This house was attached to a brick structure in 1826. In 1966 a fire destroyed the attic and second story of the brick structure. In 1967, removal of these stories was undertaken and the roof line was dropped to the first floor. At this time new shingles replaced the old slate ones. Other early stone structures still exist in Rockingham County. However, this one is unique in that the front entrance was in the gabled

---

[1] Wayland, John, *Historic Harrisonburg*, McClure Printing Company, Staunton, Virginia, 1949, p. 10.

[2] Notes from the Journals of John Wayland. Bridgewater College.

end. A number of renovations during the years have covered much of the original building's features, but the basic structure remains intact.

The house is now occupied by a local business firm as an office and is in good state of repair.

Undated photo of the Thomas Harrison House when it was General Roller's office. Note the change in roof structure before the fire.

HEDRICK HOUSE
1750

This is one of the few remaining center chimney houses to be found in the county. It is beautifully situated on a bluff overlooking the Shenandoah River.

The land on which it was built was a part of a tract of land issued to Jacob Stover in 1730. On August 17, 1749, John Hetrigh, the original spelling of the name Hedrick, purchased two hundred acres of land from John Bumgartner, building this house shortly thereafter.

Unlike most center chimney houses, where the interior is divided into two large and two small rooms, this house is unique in that the chimney is placed slightly off center, providing four unequally proportioned rooms and a separate hallway with an open staircase. There is another enclosed staircase going from the kitchen up to the large attic. The large stone chimney provides fireplaces in the large central room as well as the kitchen. The basement contains slit type windows that were common in German style houses and were probably for ventilation and fortification.

Originally a double porch served the front of this house. Four doors, two on the first floor and two on the second, opened onto this porch. These doors, plus two exterior doors on the rear of this house, made a total of six doors. This was an unusual number for this period and style.

Like many county houses, the original log house served as the nucleus for a larger house. It underwent a slight remodeling with the addition of a wing to the south. Also a gable, a bay window and another chimney were added. But, despite these changes, the original form of the house is very much in evidence. The additions enhance rather than detract.

The house remains in the Hedrick family and is in good condition.

L. to R: William Ashby Hedrick, Louise Hedrick, James C. Hedrick, Sr., James C. Hedrick Jr., Annie E. Wood Hedrick holding Laura. Woman on the porch is domestic help.

HERRINGFORD
1750

To reach this pre-Revolutionary house it was necessary to ford Cooks Creek. Because this land was owned by the Herring family, this ford was known as Herring's Ford. Thus it was natural for this house built by Alexander Herring to be called Herringford. Alexander Herring married Abigail Harrison, sister of Thomas Harrison, (see Thomas Harrison House) and came to Rockingham County in 1744 from Delaware and settled first on Linville Creek. He later moved to Cooks Creek and built this home. Alexander and Abigail had seven children. A son, Leonard, lived in this house. His daughter, Bathsheba married Captain Abraham Lincoln, making her President Abraham Lincoln's grandmother. Herringford was part of a large farm that included a servants house, gardens and orchards.

Part of this farm was Retirement, built in 1849 or 1850. It was the home of John Alexander Herring, Sr. His son was a sergeant in McClanahan's Battery in Imboden's brigade. In 1864, a Union lieutenant who was a chief engineer on Sheridan's staff was killed nearby. In retaliation, houses, in addition to barns and mills, were burned in the area. Retirement was burned. Herringford, a tenant house on the Herring property, was spared because the wife, Mrs. Valentine Bolton, showed a Union soldier her husband's Masonic papers. A guard was posted to protect the house from other details in the area.[1]

Herringford was a large log house that was weather boarded. It was built in two sections. The larger main section was rectangular in shape and had two rooms. There was not an entrance hall. Originally there was a narrow enclosed stairway to the second floor. This has been replaced with an open oak staircase with turned banisters and raised paneling. On the first floor there are two corner fireplaces and a massive, cut limestone chimney. A single fireplace is upstairs.

---

[1] Heatwole, John *The Burning; Sheridan in the Shenandoah Valley*, Rockbridge Publishing, Howell Press, Charlottesville, Virginia, pg. 98.

Old Houses in Rockingham County Revisited

The extension to the west was of equal size but not as tall. It had a two on two room arrangement with a center chimney serving the fireplaces. The basement was made of cut limestone.

Renovations to this house evolved as the Herring's wealth grew. In 1890 wainscoting was installed as well as red oak paneling. In 1897 a Dutch door with diamond patterned glass replaced the older one. The glass patterns were picked up in other windows. The house stayed in the Herring family until 1960.

Due to the dilapidated condition of the house, the owners wanted Herringford to be either torn down or moved. In 1989 the current owners purchased Herringford and decided to move the main portion of the house. The extension was in poor condition. The original cut limestones that were in the basement were reconstructed. Each stone and log was numbered and rebuilt on twenty-nine acres of wooded land in another section of Rockingham County. Herringford has come the full circle. It began as a log house that evolved into part of a large successful farm. Now that Herringford has been moved and renovated, it is a tribute to the commitment of the preservation of the past by the current residents.

Photo of Herringford being dismantled.

MARTZ-HARRISON HOUSE
1750

This house was originally the home of Michael Martz, the son of Samuel Martz. Michael Martz raised twelve children in this house. His grandson, Michael J., married Hannah Matthews, daughter of Daniel Matthews, owner of Locust Grove. In 1885, David Harrison purchased the home from Dorials Martz and his sisters, the children of Michael Martz. David Harrison was the father of J. Houston Harrison, author of *Settlers by the Long Grey Trail*, a history of the Harrison family and of Rockingham County.[1]

This house is a bank house built into a hillside. The northeast gable end is partially buried. The south gable end is elevated and above ground. It is typical of houses of this era, in that it was built in three sections. The oldest part, the north, is built of logs, now weather boarded. The remainder was constructed of weather board over frame. There are large stone chimneys at either end and a porch across the front. The house is a story and one half and now contains seven rooms,

---

[1] John W. Wayland, *Historic Homes of Northern Virginia*, Staunton, Virigina, The McClure Company, Inc. 1937, p.197.

Old Houses in Rockingham County Revisited

excluding the basement. There are two springs nearby and one is in an old stone spring house.

It is a private residence and in excellent condition.

Photo taken in 1932 by John Wayland; courtesy Handley Library, Winchester, Virginia.

Original log walls and mantel. The stove is a later addition.

Peter Paul House
c.1750

The majority of settlers following the end of the French and Indian Wars were German. English immigrants constituted a small minority of pioneer settlers in this part of the county. Most English settlers moved father south along the Shenandoah River into what is now Augusta County.

Peter Paul was one of these English settlers who located in the Dayton-Otterbine area and built this house. It is a substantial and impressive German style structure. The original house, built without a cellar, was of logs and has six rooms all centered on a large stone center chimney. This chimney can been seen in the middle of the attic. This chimney furnishes four fireplaces, two upstairs and two downstairs. A small enclosed staircase ascended to the second floor but has been replaced.

The exterior has been renovated. The logs are covered with stucco and the windows have been replaced. Nearly all of the original interior fittings survive. The "T" section of the house, built in the 1930's, contains four rooms, two up and two down. The section is divided by

a large brick chimney serving fireplaces in each of the four rooms. There is a small enclosed stairway, not the original, ascending around the chimney to the second floor. This section of the house is frame and weather boarded.

This house is a private residence and in good condition.

VLR; NRHP

Stone chimney as seen in the attic.

Undated photo before stucco was applied to the house. Photo courtesy of Seymour Paul.

MAPLEWOOD
1759

This large brick house was begun by Archibald Hopkins on a 350 acre estate. The deed originated from King George II in a 1746 patent to James Wood. It was purchased in 1755 by Robert Rollstone (Rolston), who sold it to William Castlebery the same year. William Castlebery then sold it to Archibald Hopkins in 1757. The three Hopkins brothers had migrated from New York to the Singers Glen area before 1749. Brother John's home is two miles west and is basically a twin with painted brick and an addition to the side. Brother William's home is not standing. Archibald's son, William inherited Maplewood in 1799. It then passed on to his grandson, John H. Hopkins in 1841, remaining in the Hopkins family until 1879. The property was sold to William Chrisman. In 1951, it was sold out of the Chrisman family. The current owners bought the property in 1981.

Maplewood has a Georgian exterior style. It is a large brick house with a gabled metal roof. There are two brick chimneys on each end of the house. There is a portico with five columns on the front. This house was built in three sections, giving it the appearance of two

Built in cupboards.

houses joined by a long ell. The oldest part of the house is the ell, which is one story high with two rooms and a basement. This was believed to have been built around 1759. The main part of the house was built around 1800. It is laid in Flemish bond and has a double chimney at each end. There are three rooms and hall with a stairway. The identical arrangement of rooms is on the second floor. Each room has a fireplace with a carved mantel. The mantel designs are different in every room. The rooms have built-in cupboards and hand planed shelves. The cupboard trim repeats that of the fireplace. Around 1850, another addition was built to connect to the ell. It is two stories tall and built for dining and entertaining. The second floor has two bedrooms. It is separated from the ell by a stairway. Food was carried into the dining room over these steps. Outside, original stone steps lead from the lawn to the stream below. There is a flat rock where riders dismounted from their horses.

This beautiful home has been undergoing a careful and extensive restoration since 1981. Not only has the history been thoroughly researched, but detailed records of the ongoing work are being kept.

The house is still heated with wood stoves. The wide board floors are original. Every wall that was whitewashed has been scraped to its original state with razor blades. Decorative painting below the chair rail was found in two rooms and the hall. These paintings are being restored and completed. All the windows have been removed and repaired. One pane shows the name of John H. Hopkins scratched in the glass. Samples of the layers of wall paper that have been removed are saved and recorded. There are names and drawings written on the walls, which have also been recorded.

Decorative painting.

LAIRD HOUSE
1760

This house was destroyed by fire. But the history and a 1967 photo of it is still exists. This house was situated in Lairds Knob which is located on the Massanutten Mountain. It takes its name from the Laird family who settled at its base in the middle of the eighteenth century.

James Laird, a native of Scotland, moved into the county from Lancaster County, Pennsylvania about 1756. In 1760, he purchased land from Henry Downes approximately three miles northeast of the town of Keezletown. Land survey shows that he owned 400 acres at the time of this death.

He divided this land into two tracts that were separated by a creek and willed them to his two sons, James and David. The house photographed here was located on the lower tract of this property and was willed to David Laird.

It was a substantially built log house with four rooms and a loft. The rooms were divided by upright pine boards set in tongue and groove and fitted to each other. Inside walls were plastered. Interior doors still had their original hinges and a few locks remained.

The outstanding feature of this house was the large stone chimney on the east side. It was five feet thick and seventeen feet long. It was constructed of random laid limestone and served two large fireplaces. There was a chimney in the back room that was probably added at a later date. There was a small cellar under the west portion of the house with dirt floor and a heavy reinforced door.

The house and land remained in the Laird family until 1854. It was privately owned at the time of the fire.

LETHE
1760

Peachy Ridgeway Gilmer was the son of Dr. George Gilmer of Williamsburg. He and his wife, Mary Meriweather of Albemarle came to this location on the Shenandoah River about 1760. Lethe, which means the place where all is forgotten, was built in the English style that was prevalent in Williamsburg. Peachy Gilmer was very well connected socially and politically. He wanted a house suitable for entertaining and raising a family. This house was considered very modern for the time since a central chimney house plan was more common. He was probably the first area resident to have a house with a center hall and a dining room.

Peachy Gilmer had two sons and four daughters. Thomas, the oldest, married Elizabeth Lewis, daughter of Thomas Lewis of Lynnwood and moved to the state of Georgia. Their son, George Rockingham Gilmer married Frances Grattan and later became governor of the state of Georgia. Their daughter, Elizabeth married Robert Grattan of Contentment.

Lethe is built of brick in Flemish bond with a limestone foundation. The floor plan is a three over three. There is a center hallway with open staircase ascending to the attic. The attic or third floor of this house is quite spacious. It is said that slaves were quartered in the rooms in this section, and a special staircase was constructed down the back of the building for their use. There is a full basement with a cook fireplace on the west end. Two end chimneys provide fireplaces for all the main rooms.[1]

The house has been remodeled and added onto during the years, although the woodwork in the original structure is intact. None of the once existing out buildings remain.

Lethe remained in the Gilmer family for several generations. It is privately owned and is abandoned.

---

[1]Senior Thesis by Richard D. F. Martin, Special Collections, James Madison Library, Harrisonburg, Virginia.

Old Houses in Rockingham County Revisited

WINFIELD
1760

The first family to live in the original log section of this frontier house was a German-speaking Click family. In 1814 the Clicks sold the property to John Horman who later sold it to George Showalter. Dr. Richard Winfield bought the property in 1829 and moved in with his wife Elizabeth Salvage and their children. The place was eventually inherited by their oldest son, Dr. John Quincy Winfield. Dr. John Q. Winfield married Sarah "Sallie" Neff. They had three children. Sons were Charles, who became a lawyer, and Turner Ashby, who became the first mayor of Miami, Florida. The Winfields' daughter, Paulina, "Miss Lina," became a published poet and popular piano teacher. Dr. and Mrs. Winfield also raised an adopted daughter, Antoinette Massie. Charles and Paulina, neither of whom married, occupied the house throughout their lives.

In 1859 at Cootes Store, Dr. Winfield gathered together a band of men who called themselves the Letcher-Brocks Gap Rifles, named after Virginia's governor and the area of Rockingham County that was their home. At the beginning of the Civil War, this unit enlisted as a mounted company in the Seventh Virginia Cavalry, commanded by Turner Ashby, and fully participated in "Stonewall" Jackson's famous Valley Campaign of 1862. Captain Winfield was commander of Company B of Ashby's Cavalry and exhibited military talent and courage. He became a hero during the taking of the depot at Buckton Station near Front Royal. After his horse was shot from underneath him, he led a squad of men into the fortified building and engaged in hand-to-hand combat with Union soldiers. Winfield emerged carrying the Federal flag.[1] After the death of General Ashby, Captain Winfield was mentioned as his successor. However, due to a health condition, Winfield was forced to return to civilian life.

In 1864, Winfield was active once more. While the group of partisans he had organized raided Sheridan's supply trains, Federal soldiers under Colonel Thomas Devine searched Captain Winfield's home in hopes of capturing him. The large mill on the property was burned, but the Winfield home was spared.[2]

The original log portion of the house is a fine example of a German style center chimney structure, built in a three over three plan. The large and complex central chimney serves five fireplaces. The triangular shape of the chimney becomes rectangular before exiting the roof. Rooms have plastered walls and chair rail. There is an outside door for each room on the first floor. A circular staircase ascends from the first floor to the attic. A small cellar is located under part of the original house. Some of the original hinges and locks remain. Dr. Winfield constructed a frame addition to the north side of the house, doubling its size. This addition also has a staircase to the attic. In 1870 the ground floor room of the addition was the meeting place for the families, led by Dr. and Mrs. Winfield, that founded the local Presbyterian Church.

After Paulina's death in 1950, the house was willed to the Town of Broadway. The town's plans to use the structure were abandoned in 1972. The house is now privately owned and is undergoing restoration.

---

[1] Tanner, Robert, *Stonewall in the Valley*. Doubleday & Company, Inc. Garden City, New York. p. 210.

[2] Heatwole, John, *The Burning: Sheridan in the Shenandoah Valley*. Rockbridge Publishing. Charlottesville, Virginia. pp. 125-126, 139-140.

LEWIS ZIRKLE
1760

One of the most primitive stone houses to be found in Rockingham County is this house built by Lewis Zirkle, Sr. in 1760. It offers a great deal of interest, architecturally, in that it retains most of its Germanic central chimney design.

The Zirkle family had its origin in Germany, coming to Pennsylvania about 1725. In 1760 Lewis Zirkle, Sr. settled on Smith's Creek while his brother, Peter, moved on to Bototourt County. Lewis Zirkle was a tanner and a miller and pursued both operations near his home. His son, Lewis Zirkle, Jr. was also a tanner and miller and he continued his father's operations in the same location.

This house is the first of the Zirkle houses built on Smith's Creek. The house is simply but sturdily built of randomly laid field stone built against a bank so that the first floor is partially below ground. At one time it was enlarged on the west side with a long structure which has been torn down, apparently taking with it the west end stone wall and chimney.

It contains four rooms, two on the first or ground level and two on the second which is also on ground level in the rear.

Across the front is a double porch with steps leading into each floor. There is an exterior door on the back. On the second level, there are two windows on the back and front. On the ground level the windows are narrow and horizontal with wooden bars.[1]

It was impossible to examine the interior of this house thoroughly, but it is felt that it is original.

Close to the house stands the remains of a stone structure, built at a later date. This could have been used as a cook or wash house.

This house has been empty for many years and it is difficult to inspect.

Rear of the house.

---

[1] United States Government, Works Progress Administration, "Historical American Buildings Survey, Rockingham County, 1935-1939," Virginia State Library, Richmond, Virginia, Photographic Files, unbound, uncataloged.

EMANUEL SUTER HOUSE
1767

William Sample built the original house in 1767, on land that was granted by King George III for services rendered. But, because of a trip to England, William Sample, in turn, forfeited it to William Dunlap. When William Dunlap went west, the land and house came into the possession of Peter Swope. Swope's daughter married Emanuel Suter, and they took possession of the house in 1855. The house stayed in the Suter family for two hundred years.

The Suter family was of German descent and were Mennonites. They came to this country from France about 1811-1813. They settled in Pennsylvania and later came to the Shenandoah Valley about 1815.

Emanuel Suter was a potter and made crocks and jars for household use. Many

Emanuel Suter

pieces of Suter pottery can still be found in the community. During the Civil War, he also made dishes for table use. Pieces of Suter pottery are now collectors' items. The pottery was torn down in 1893.

Examples of Suter pottery.

Emanuel Suter was one of the first to serve as a member of the board of trustees when the public school system was organized in Virginia after the Civil War.

Pottery.

This log house, now weather boarded, consists of four rooms, two on the first floor with an enclosed staircase leading to two rooms on the second floor. The original stone chimney serviced fireplaces in the first and second floor west rooms. The downstairs fireplace was large enough for cooking. This chimney has been torn down. The interior log walls have been plastered and are original. Dividing walls are of tongue and groove upright pine boards. All doors are original four paneled type made of pine. The windows are the original six over nine panes on the first floor with six over six panes on the second. In 1874, the house was remodeled to add an ell to the north side. At this time, an outdoor bake oven was also built but it no longer stands. A second chimney was added to the east side. Outside is a limestone well house built by William Sample at an unknown date. In this well house there are plastered ceilings probably for fireproofing. In 1882, Mr. Suter built another house on this property. This was used for his sons to live in when they married.

This home is a private residence and in good condition.

Limestone well house.

John Rice House
1776

John Rice came into the area of Honey Run in 1770. He first built a log cabin. Then he left for Culpeper to select a bride. Mary Finney returned with him in 1776. Between 1775-1779 he replaced his log cabin with a two story weather boarded frame house. John Rice was a Justice of Rockingham County Court and was a very well-to-do man. At the time of his death, he owned 950 acres. He died in 1804 and his wife continued to live in this house until her death in 1824. This house remained in the Rice family until 1884.[1]

In Williamsburg, John Rice had seen frame houses which were painted. He wanted to repeat this idea in his own house. The weather boarding was six inches wide and more than one-half-inch thick with ornamental beading on the edges. Hand wrought nails were used to nail the weather boards in place. There is now vinyl siding over the exterior. This solid, well made frame house has mortise and tenon joints. The original house was two rooms over two with a center hall.

Yellow pine was used for the woodwork including the floors and

---

[1] Deed book 44, p.244, Rockingham Courthouse, Harrisonburg, Virginia.

Old Houses in Rockingham County Revisited

mantels. The interior doors are four paneled with wide cross bars. There is a flat hand rail treatment along the steps in the front hall.[2]

The current owners purchased this home in 1978 and began remodeling in 1985. A poorly made lean-to addition was removed. A kitchen and upstairs bedroom were added. Because the original front door was in disrepair, the current owner made a reproduction of the six paneled door from lumber found in the house. Replastering was done in the original style. All the floors are original with the exception of one room. Here the floor boards were in poor condition and they were replaced. The original front porch has been replaced with a wider, more practical style.

Hand rail treatment.

Behind the property is a cemetery. It has a brick four-foot wall with

a wrought iron gate. There is a potential for twelve graves here but there are only eight now. The most recent burial was a family member in 1995. Until then, the last family member was buried in 1885. Mysteriously, John Rice himself is buried at Dayton Cemetery. Today this house is a private residence and is in excellent condition.

Example of the woodwork is seen in this mantel from the north first floor room.

---

[2] May, CE, *Life Under Four Flags in North River Basin of Virginia*, p. 210.

Mannheim

c. 1779

Mannheim is a large stone and frame house. Even though the builder and exact date of construction have been controversial, current restoration has yielded some clues. The rubble stone construction, woodwork and recent discovery of an indoor cooking fireplace put the date around 1770. Sources credit Michael Coffman (Kauffman) with construction of the stone part. The frame addition was probably built in 1855.

Mannheim was named after the German city from where the Coffmans formerly originated. This home was part of a large 360-acre plantation. There was constant visiting and entertaining here. At mealtimes, three tables were set; one for the family with imported china; one for the white hired help and one for the slaves. In the attic was a long narrow board shaped like a coffin on which the dead, both white and black were laid out.[1] The Coffmans were originally Men-

---

[1] Carrie Esther Spencer, Bernard Samuels, Walter Berry Samuels, *A Civil War Marriage*, Boyce Virginia, Carr Publishing Company Inc., 1956, p.63.

nonites, but after becoming slave owners, they fell out of favor with the church. Michael Coffman was a breeder and seller of slaves. Across the road are the remains of slave quarters. These building are in need of repair, but it is evident that they consist of two separate rooms. There are enclosed chimneys and each fireplace has a built in cupboard next to it.

The original portion of the house, which is almost square, is two stories high with a large center chimney. Each floor originally was partitioned with tongue and groove upright pine boards into two large and two small rooms. Each of the large rooms has a fireplace with mantel. There are two enclosed staircases leading to the second floor. One of these continues to the attic. The second floor is partitioned into rooms like those on the first floor with a fireplace and mantel in the larger room. All doors are original. When the frame extension on the west side was added in 1855, it made a total of twelve rooms in the house. Dr. Samuel Coffman, Michael's son, had his office in a small building on the property near the kitchen. It still exists and has

Photo taken in 1958. Photographer unknown.

been stabilized. Dr. Coffman lived across the road in the house now called the Isaac Wenger house.

The current owners have completed renovation of the frame section. Work is in progress on the older portion. Their most significant discovery was the 6' x 5' indoor cooking fireplace in the large first floor north room. This was behind a fireplace which the owners were having difficulty getting operational. Also, the current woodwork and trim were simply nailed over the original trim. The front porch, which was added later, has been removed. The rear porch has been enclosed for more living area.

This house is an excellent condition and maintained as a private residence.

Fireplace that was discovered during renovations.

1900 postcard.

CONRAD'S STORE
c. 1812

One of the oldest store buildings in Rockingham County stands not far from the place where Governor Spotswood crossed the Shenandoah River in 1716. At that time, before the town of Elkton was formed, the settlement there was known as Elk Run Valley.

The Stephen Conrad family was of German descent that came to the Shenandoah Valley from Pennsylvania about 1750. During his life, Stephen Conrad bought hundreds of acres of land and also operated several businesses from his plantation at East Point. He became a Captain in the Revolutionary War and guarded the road leading to Swift Run Gap.

Captain Conrad and his wife had three sons. The second son was George and in 1810 he married Susanna Miller, who was descended from Adam Miller. About 1812 he built this structure from logs. It was known as Conrad's Store. George and his wife lived on the second floor and ran the store below. On April 6, 1816, Conrad's Store was the area's first post office with George Conrad as the first postmaster. He later built a home on the Shenandoah River. After he resigned as postmaster in 1832, he moved to Harrisonburg. He was the first person to be buried in Woodbine Cemetery.

The main part of the house is of logs and is now weather boarded and sealed. There were no fireplaces; chimneys were built for stoves. There are heavy shutters with iron bars extending diagonally across the windows and secured with large bolts. There is a front porch across the full length of the house. One enclosed staircase leads to the second floor. The windows are six over six paned and believed to be original.

This structure is now vacant.

1932 Photo taken by the Historic American Building Survey; courtesy the Library of Virginia, Richmond, Virginia.

Old Houses in Rockingham County Revisited

KEEZLE HOUSE
c. 1790

This substantial stone house is a landmark in the town of Keezletown. It is a slightly rectangular house with interior end chimneys. It remains today as it was originally, except for the addition of a front porch and a small extension to the rear.

It is difficult to date this house. George Keezle bought 566 acres of land in 1780. He set aside 100 acres for the town of Keezell (Keezletown) With the sale of each lot, the buyer had to agree to build a house. On February 23, 1784 George Keezle sold the property this house is on to Thomas Lounsdale. He, in turn, sold it nine months later to Jacob Spoths. There is no deed of sale, but Spoths owned this property for fourteen years. It is assumed that in order to keep the property he had to build a house on it. Spoths sold the property to

Keezle House is on the right. Undated photo.

Michael Crobarger to pay off a debt. Crobarger sold a stone house to Henry Keezle, the son of George, in 1805.

There are six rooms and the interior is very plain with simple mantels and woodwork. It is a basic three over three plan. It is a combination of English and German styles. The first floor has one large room, a kuche, running the width of the house. In this room is the largest fireplace in the house as it was used for cooking. There is a center hall with exterior doors at each end. There are two smaller rooms con-

Fireplace in the kuche.

Dove tail chair rail.

necting off the hallway. The front room is called the stube or best room These rooms share a double corner chimney. Each room has its own fireplace. Stairs from the kuche ascend to the second floor where there is one unusually large room with a fireplace. This room is flanked by two smaller rooms. There is a small fireplace in one of these rooms. The mantels and floors are original. An interesting feature in the large room is the original dove tail chair rail. The window sills are eighteen inches deep. Evidence of a split wood roof can be seen underneath the tin roof. The attic has pegged and numbered beams. There is a half cellar with a dirt floor. Here it is evident that the first floor is supported by eleven log beams. They were hewn only on the top to support the floor. Some of the bark still remains. The well is original and operational.

This house has had numerous owners and probably as many interior changes which also contribute to the lack of an exact date. The current owner has lived here since 1988 and is in the process of renovation.

BIBLER HOUSE
1793

The Biblers were early settlers who migrated from Pennsylvania. They built this substantial gray limestone house in 1793. The house bears a chimney plate with the name of Lewis Bibler, his wife, Barbara, and the date 1793. Lewis Bibler lived in this house until he died in 1848.

This house stands over a spring. It was built in sections and the exterior walls are eighteen inches thick. The exterior is plain and it is oblong in shape. A porch runs across the east side and the house is only one room deep. Most of the windows are original. A spring house with arched doorways leading into the basement area existed on the west side, but it has been removed.

This house has been converted into apartments and inspection of the interior was not possible.

CONTENTMENT
1793

This home is significant not only because of the substantial size but also because it is one of the first homes of the Grattan family in Virginia. Contentment was built in 1793 by Robert Grattan. His father, John, owned the land. John immigrated from Ireland and was a miller by trade. In 1769, he had a store, log cabin and one of the first flour mills in the Shenandoah Valley. John Grattan was a member of the Virginia House of Delegates and one of the justices appointed for Rockingham County at its formation in 1777. During the Revolutionary War, John was a lieutenant in the Continental Army.

Robert Grattan married Elizabeth Gilmer, daughter of Peachy Gilmer of Lethe. All four of Robert's sons served in the Civil War. Robert and Peter lost their lives. Charles and George, who were Confederate officers, survived to become judges. George inherited Contentment. In 1867, Robert's daughter, Lucy, married Confederate captain George Chrisman of the Third Battalion of the Virginia Reserves.

There is a family graveyard at Contentment with tombstones of many Grattan family members.

During the Civil War, General John D. Imboden, commanding officer of the Valley Brigade, set up his headquarters at Contentment in 1864. On June 4, 1864, he met with Brigadier General William E. Jones. They were planning their confrontation with US Army General David Hunter. At this time there were many troops camping on the grounds of Contentment. One of these troops was the Boy Company, commanded by Captain Chrisman. On June 5, General Jones was killed at the battle of Piedmont.[1]

On September 26, Sheridan sent infantry brigades to Contentment to keep a path open for calvary returning from Augusta County. Because of Mrs. Grattan's status as a widow, the outbuildings were not burned. It is fortunate that the soldiers did not know that her sons and future son-in-law were Confederate soldiers.[2]

Decorative lintel.

Contentment is an unusually large house for this period. The brick is locally fired and is laid in Flemish bond. The four chimneys serve nine fireplaces. Most windows contain the original glass and are nine over nine. The lintels are fluted and have decorative button designs at the top corners. The present porches are not original. The bay windows were also added later.

On the first floor there are four rooms with five on the second floor. A wide center hall runs the depth of the house. The staircase is

[1] Brice, Marshall M., *Conquest of a Valley*, The University of Virginia Press, Charlottesville, Virginia, 1965, p.40.

[2] Heatwole, John, *The Burning, Sheridan in the Shenandoah Valley*, Rockbridge Publishing, Howell Press, Inc., Charlottesville, Virginia, 1998, p.51.

most unusual in that it ascends from the rear of this hall as a box staircase A smaller enclosed staircase continues from the second floor hall up to the attic. The second floor has thirteen foot ceilings and four bedrooms. Later owners divided a fifth bedroom for use as two bathrooms. Also, the bedrooms were altered to add closets.

One of eight different mantels.

There are eight mantels in the house. Each has a different design. There is a flush chair rail in all the rooms. The first floor hall features a flush railing about seven feet high into which are mounted metal brackets six inches long. The Grattans probably hung their chairs there when they were entertaining.

The current owners purchased this house in 1968. It is in excellent condition as a private residence.

1932 photo of Contentment taken by John Waylaid; courtesy Bridgewater College, Bridgewater, Virginia.

STANLEY HOUSE
1795

The Stanley house is situated on sixteen acres near the top of Dean Mountain, a part of the Blue Ridge Range. When one finally reaches this point one can thoroughly appreciate the uncanny sense that directed the early settlers to a particular building site. Here, at this elevation the mountain levels off into a series of cleared areas, dependable springs abound and the soil is fertile enough to support a substantial farm community. The people who settled in these isolated areas depended upon the land for their survival and built their home out of the material close at hand.

The placement of windows, the use of an inside chimney and the ingenious utilization of the terrain make this house an outstanding example of early county construction. The approach from the front or east side of the house gives it the appearance of being the usual two storied house with porch. From the rear or west side the basement level is exposed making it actually a three-storied house. The first floor is divided into two rooms, one larger than the other. The walls are a combination of field stone and exposed log. Originally the smaller room was used for storage and had a dirt floor. The larger room had a wood floor, with a fireplace—it was used as a general purpose room.

A narrow, enclosed staircase ascends to the second floor which is divided by vertical pine boards into two rooms. The room on the north side has a door which opens onto the porch on the east side. In these two rooms the walls were plastered. The staircase continues to the third floor, which is similarly divided into two rooms, making a total of six rooms. The walls are exposed logs.

The site, originally consisting of 400 acres, was patented to John Stanley in 1794 by Governor Henry Lee. It is assumed that John Stanley built the house shortly thereafter. It remained in the Stanley family until 1842, when it was sold by his son, Jonathan, who had moved to Missouri.

The property changed hands many times until 1966 when it was purchased by the current owners. The house had not been occupied for thirty years and was in bad shape. The original vertical weather boarding has been removed from the west side exposing the primitive hand hewn logs. The basement floor has been converted into comfortable living quarters. This house remains in its original state as an unusual mountain farm house.

Photo taken of interior October 12, 1978; courtesy of the Daily News Record, Harrisonburg, Virginia.

Baxter House
c. 1800

The use of log for the construction of houses, barns and outbuildings was prevalent during this period in the county, due to the availability of the material and the need for quick, inexpensive housing. A large number of these structures remain, many of them still hidden under weather boarding.

An outstanding and unusual example of log construction is known as the Baxter house. While it is difficult to date a log house, it is safe to assume that this one was built at the end of the eighteenth century or early in the nineteenth. It was built in two sections; the original section being a two story, two room house with a limestone chimney, a large fireplace and a boxed staircase.

The shape of the chimney is unusual in that it is quite large on the first floor and tapers to a very narrow section at the second story. The logs in this section are V notched and chinked with stone and wood.

Enlargement of a log house was accomplished by several methods. Usually another "crib" or rectangular structure was built in line with the original house and a passage was left between. This was known as a "dog trot" and this space was generally covered by the common roof of the two structures. In the case where the entire building was later covered with boarding the passageway became a hall or another room.

In some examples of enlargement, a second "crib" was constructed against the first with the two exterior walls, back to back, forming a two log thick interior wall. A door was cut through the two walls and the house was increased in size by two more rooms. A porch was generally constructed across the front and both first floor rooms opened onto it. Porches were a vital part of the house and served an important function as work and storage areas.

The Baxter house is unique in that the enlargement was not accomplished by either of these methods. Instead, the new logs were spliced into the existing ones so there is an interior wall which is only one log thick. The corner timbering in the newer section is fully dovetailed and the logs have been carefully squared and fitted.

The house was further enlarged by the addition of a lean-to added to the rear making it a seven room house. The entire structure was then covered with batten boards which have now been removed from the main structure and the beauty of log construction is revealed.

Records show that the Baxter family settled on Linville Creek and acquired large amounts of land. By 1789 George Baxter is reported as possessing over one thousand acres of land. George A. Baxter, his son, was president of Washington College, now Washington and Lee University, from 1799 to 1829.

The house and land have remained in the same family. It is in excellent condition as a private residence.

VLR; NRHP

Blue Ball Tavern
c 1800

Prior to the construction of the Valley Turnpike, 1834-1846, the most frequented road running north and south through the Valley was the Keezletown Road, which followed an old Indian trail along the west side of the Massanutten Mountain. At various intervals along this road were taverns and stagecoach stops. At these places fresh horses could be obtained, as well as food and drink and sometimes lodging for the night.

One such place was known as "The Blue Ball Tavern." Its sign was a ball of cast iron, about eighteen inches in diameter, hollow and painted blue. Above the large ball was a smaller one, of glass, about six inches in diameter.

The tavern was the home place of David Harnett and was later occupied by the Flook Family who were probably the tavern keepers.[1]

---

[1] John W. Wayland, "Wayside Taverns," Daily News Record, June 12 1953, Rockingham Public Library, Microfilm file, Harrisonburg, Virginia.

It is an imposing structure, even today, although the sign has long disappeared and the cast iron fence which once surrounded it no longer stands. The front portion of the house is almost square, two stories high fronted with a two column portico with balcony. A two storied extension runs to the back with double porch along the south side. Four large brick chimneys provide fireplaces in each room. There is a center hallway running through the main portion of the house, with a charming circular staircase rising from it.

It is a private residence and in very good condition.

Left to Right: Francis Flook Yancey, Minnie Yancey Armentrout; On Porch: Margaret Sellars Flook; Picture: George W. Yancey; Righ: Nanny Yancey Hulvey, Elizabeth Ann Flook and Black Will.

This photo is undated but was probably taken by a traveling photographer. Since Mr. Yancey was dead, the family simply placed his portrait outside to be included in the family photo.

BONNYBROOK

c.1800

This was the home of the McGahey family for whom the town of McGaheysville was named. It is located near the town on a small stream called Bonny Brook. The house was built by Tobias R. McGahey and stands on the site of an earlier log house. About 1850 W.T. McGahey began to manufacture various articles and implements of wood and iron, such as door latches and locks, ditching machines, corn harvesters and machines for cleaning seeds. During the Civil War he made swords and gun parts. The massive grindstone on which swords were finished and sharpened is still preserved.[1]

It is a large brick house, built on the three over three plan with a long extension to the west. There is a center hallway with open stairway. There is another enclosed stairway in the extension. The house is in excellent condition and is maintained as a private residence.

---

[1] United States Government, Works Progress Administration, Historical American Buildings Survey, Rockingham County, 1935-1939, Virginia State Library, Richmond, Virginia, Photographic files.

Grindstone used to make swords.

THE CEDARS

c. 1800

This excellent example of a frame house with siding is a salt box style house. At one time it sat in a grove of magnificent cedar trees which gave it its name.

Although it appears small, it is in fact rather spacious having a center hall with open stairway and two rooms on either side of the hall each with fireplaces. The second floor, which is a three quarter story, has the same arrangement without fireplaces.

The back one story extension is composed of three rooms, now converted into a bathroom, utility room and porch room.

An interesting feature of the exterior of this house is the cornice treatment of the windows. Originally solid shutters fitted beneath these cornices but have been removed.

This house was at one time the home of Dr. William H. Ruffner. He was an eminent scientist and educator. He was the first State

Superintendent of Public Instruction under the new constitution, serving from 1870 to 1882. Also, he was the first President of the first state normal school at Farmville, VA, 1884-1887. [1]

Dr. Ruffner was married to Harriet Ann Grey, the daughter of Robert Grey, well known lawyer of Harrisonburg and builder of "Collicello," a beautiful old home which formerly stood near the intersection of North Liberty and Gay Streets. Mr. Grey held extensive land holdings as well as being a popular lawyer.

This house is in poor condition and uninhabited.

---

[1] Wayland, John, *Historic Harrisonburg*, McClure Printing Company, Staunton, Virginia, 1949, pp 77-81.

COURT MANOR
c.1800

The original part of this house was built by Reuben Moore about the end of the eighteenth century. The house is a large two storied brick house. There were twelve rooms, all with fireplaces. The rooms are spacious with large windows opening onto the vistas which surround it. There is a center hall with open reverse staircase running from back to front. The exterior is enhanced with a four column portico and a double porch extending along the back ell section which was a twentieth century addition.

In 1925 this house and farm were purchased by Dr. Willis Sharpes Kilmer, who developed it into a show place, expanding the house and gardens to their present proportions. He used the farm for the breeding and training of fine race horses known world wide.[1]

Dr. Willis Sharpes Kilmer

[1] Personal interview, Mr. Thomas Harrison, April 1968

After Dr. Kilmer died, Court Manor was sold and used for various ventures over the years. When the current owners purchased this home, they did an extensive renovation and have returned this home and grounds to a showplace status.

Undated photo showing the house and barns. Courtesy of Mrs. Andrew Yancey.

Photo taken in 1936 by Kaylor of Harrisonburg, authorized by Dr. Kilmer, for use in a publication by John Wayland.

61

RODHAM KEMPER HOUSE

c. 1800

This house is located in the town of Cross Keys. It was once known as the Cross Keys Tavern and had a sign of crossed keys hung over its door.

This house was built to be used as a tavern about 1800. The Cross Keys post office was established in this building in 1804. J. Hancock was the first postmaster, leaving his name cut in the weather boarding.

Rodham Kemper moved here in 1823 and ran a store from 1823 to 1845. During the Civil War the house was used as a hospital while the battle of Cross Keys was being fought.[1]

The main portion of the house is a rectangular plan, weather-boarded, with large stone end chimneys that were partially exposed. Eight rooms are in the main section. A three room extension runs to the back. It is one story high giving the house a "T" shape.

It is felt that this extension, which was weather boarded log, was at one time a large dining room. One room in the front part of the house showed signs of a partitioned off section used as the bar.

This house is in poor condition.

Vernon Meyerhoffer in front of the house. Undated photo.

[1] John W. Wayland, "Wayside Tavern," *Daily News Record*, June 12, 1953, Rockingham Public Library, Microfilm file, Harrisonburg, Virginia

KRATZER HOUSE
c. 1800

One of the loveliest and most carefully preserved 18th century farm-houses in Rockingham County is the old Kratzer homestead. It was built by Joseph Kratzer on land which was sold to him by Jacob Coffman in 1784. The original owner was Christian Kratzer. There were originally 3000 acres surrounding this home. The exact date of construction has not been established but it is believed to be around 1800.[1] Local stories say that Joseph Kratzer took about twelve years to build this house. He lived in a log house nearby. There was also a stone barn and fort on this property. Another large barn and granary

---

[1] United States Government Works, Progress Administration, Historical American Buildings Survey, Rockingham County, 1935-1939, Virginia State Library, Richmond, Virginia

Example of a mantel.

were burned by Union Soldiers during the Civil War.

It is a large house built of limestone. The main portion is two stories high with four rooms on the first floor and four on the second. The first floor rooms are of almost equal size, while the second floor rooms vary in size. There is a trap door in one of the downstairs rooms, that was used for hiding valuables. There is a center hall with the original front and rear doors. An open staircase ascends from this hallway to the attic. Wheat was originally stored in the attic before the barn was built. Evidence of that is shown in the wear of the treads of the stairs and grain in the grooves of wood. Original pegs are in the wall of the hall and were probably used for hanging coats. Each room has a different style fireplace and mantel. There is another small enclosed service stairway in the west first floor room. The steps are very narrow and they are enclosed with a small board and batten door. First floor windows are nine over nine pine frame windows. Six over nine paned windows are featured upstairs. The floor is original on the second floor and is made of pine.

Two sun rooms were later added to the front of the house. Also, a one

Service stairway.

and half story addition was built on the south end. On the main floor is a large room that is now used as a kitchen. Stairs off this room descend to the original cooking kitchen. The fireplace in the old kitchen is 6' x 5'. Storage shelves are built into the back wall and there are also hidden shelves behind the wall. A door leads outside to the cellar.

One of the many interesting features of this house is this large cellar which is built under a portion of the main structure. This room, which is only partially underground has very thick whitewashed stone walls and an arched ceiling. The floor is brick. The door is horizontally split and it has the original wrought iron bolts.

This house is an excellent condition and is maintained as a private residence.

Large cook fireplace.

Cellar.

LINCOLN HOMESTEAD
c. 1800

In 1768 John Lincoln, his wife, five sons and four daughters moved from Berks County, Pennsylvania into the Shenandoah Valley, where he bought six hundred acres of land on Linville Creek. His eldest son, Abraham, who married in Rockingham County, was the father of Thomas Lincoln, who was born on Linville Creek in 1776. In 1783, Abraham with his family, including Thomas, later the father of the President, migrated to Kentucky. Abraham's father, known as "Virginia John," remained on Linville Creek.

The ten room house was built in two sections. The first block, built by Captain Jacob Lincoln, consisted of three rooms down and three rooms up with fireplaces in each room.

The second block was built by his son, Colonel Abraham Lincoln, in 1842. This was a separate four room house and for many years was not permanently connected with the main house. In later years it was bricked in, and the house took on its present appearance.

Jacob Lincoln hauled fine mahogany lumber from New York or

Pennsylvania and had a cabinet maker by the name of Schultz make it into fine furniture for his home. It is thought that Schultz also decorated and made the fine mantel in the southwest room and the front door entrance, which is of unusual beauty. The mantels have been removed from the house, and only the doorway remains to testify to Mr. Schultz's skill.

In May of 1874, the heirs of Colonel Abraham Lincoln sold the farm and house to Mr. Michael Bowman. It was Mr. Bowman who connected the two houses permanently.

Nearby, on the hill, is the Lincoln cemetery, now occupied by five generations of the family.[1]

The Lincoln Homestead is privately owned.

VLR; NRHP

Doorway

---

[1] John W. Wayland, *The Lincolns in Virginia*, Staunton, Virginia, The McClure Printing Company, 1946, p.84.

MAUZY HOUSE
c. 1800

This imposing structure was built in an area once known as "Spartopolis". Tradition has it that it was once a stop on the old stage line which traveled through the Valley. Hays Tavern was also located at this crossroads along with stores and shops and other buildings. The area was a small town center. Also on this property is a general store that was built in 1836. Other buildings are a lock up, spring house and school.

This house was built by William Pickering. He was a Scotch-Irish inden-

Spring house.

tured servant to Jacob Woodley. William Pickering married Jacob Woodley's daughter Barbara. It came into the Mauzy family by marriage in 1872. The Mauzy's were Huguenots migrating from Charleston, South Carolina to Stafford County, Virginia and then into the Shenandoah Valley.

The house is a large frame house covered by siding. The plan of this house is six rooms over six. The south section has a center chimney which serviced two back to back fireplaces on the first floor and two others on the second floor. Only one of these second floor fireplaces remains. There are built in chimney closets by these fireplaces on both floors. The two rooms on either end run the depth of the building and have fireplaces. The north room is a more formal keep-

Warming fireplace in the keeping room.

Entry staircase.

ing room with a warming fireplace. The chimney on the south end is placed in front of the ridge, indicating that it could have been an earlier construction.[1]

Inside the main door is an entrance hall with a staircase that goes to a landing and turns to the second floor. There is grain painting on all the mantels and doors.. The door latches, floors and windows are original. The walls are plastered as well as the ceiling on the second floor. There is a full basement with a flagstone floor and exposed log supports.

A double porch runs the length of the front of the building with a one story porch crossing the back. It has been remodeled, to some extent, through the years, but most of it is the original structure. There is a general store on the site that was built in 1836.

The Mauzy House was converted into an apartment. Now it has been converted into shops that sells antiques and gifts.

Example of grain painting on a mantel.

---

[1] Houston-Harrison, *Settlers by the Long Grey Trail*, Dayton, Virginia, Joseph K. Ruebush-Elkins Company, 1935, p.516

General Store.

Photograph taken by John Wayland around 1932 titled Tavern on Valley Turnpike; courtesy of Handley Library, Winchester, Virginia.

Old Houses in Rockingham County Revisited

NICHOLAS HOUSE
1800

The land here was a survey of 460 acres to Jacob Nicholas dated May 11, 1771. It was a part of a tract purchased by Christopher Francisco from Jacob Stover and conveyed to Jacob Nicholas by Ludowidk Francisco. In June, 1794, the land was divided between two sons, Peter and Jacob Nicholas. The portion containing the house was inherited by Jacob. In this division a house is mentioned and it can only be assumed that this refers to the present house.

This house is an excellent example of the size of some of the log houses built in the county during this period. It measures forty eight feet wide and thirty feet deep and contains ten rooms. It was built on the three over three plan with a center hall and end chimneys of limestone.

The basement was originally used for cooking and storage, with a large fireplace in the south room. The first floor is divided into three rooms: one large room on the south side, which has an inside chimney measuring nine feet wide and five feet deep, and two rooms on the north side with corner fireplaces. There is an open staircase ascending from the wide center hall, to the attic. The second floor is divided into four rooms with three fireplaces.

Interior walls are plastered with chair rails and clothes boards. Doors, hinges and locks are original as are some of the mantels. Exterior walls have the original weather boarding and the roof is the original imported English tin.

In 1862 it becomes, by inheritance, the property of Albert P. Nicholas who in 1887 sold it to Benjamin F. Jackson. It is currently owned by a fourth generation member of the Jackson family. It is in good condition as a private residence.

RIVERBANK
c. 1800

This was the home of Colonel William Burbridge Yancey (1803-1858) and later the home of his son, Captain William Benjamin Yancey (1836-1912). It is one of the many imposing houses which were built along the south fork of the Shenandoah River prior to the Civil War. This is flat bottom land, highly productive and conducive to successful farming.

Colonel William Yancey owned a large tract of land in this area and was an officer in the colonial militia. He was also a Justice of the Peace and was elected to the Virginia Legislature, 1849-50 and 1851-53. He was twice

Captain William Benjamin Yancey

married, his first wife being Mary Kyle Smith, daughter of William Smith of "Smithland". His second wife was Mary Gibbons, daughter of John Gibbons of nearby "Locus Dale." "Captain Billy" was an extensive land owner, successful farmer, merchant and miller. Serving with the Virginia Volunteer Infantry during the Civil War until 1864, he was wounded at the battle of Winchester. He reared a family of ten children and his descendants have kept a continuing interest in this house.

L to R Captain Billy Yancey on the horse, his mother, Mary Smith Yancey, on the porch, his wife, Victoria Winborough Yancey beside the porch.

A large brick structure built in the shape of a T, it is similar in style to the other large Federal river houses of this period. It has an awkward grace which sets it apart and gives it a distinct style all its own. Originally the road followed the river so that what is now the rear of the house was the main entrance. This part of the house had a double porch with large circular columns. The river had barge traffic and there was a ford just below the house so this offered a fine view. From this porch the front door opened into a small hallway with open staircase ascending to the second floor. The second floor has three large rooms and a hallway with a landing for the stairs. Two of the rooms have side by side fireplaces, which kept a fire going at night and one ready for the morning. The third room has a door leading to a large porch.

A driveway continued around the house to the east side where guests alighted onto a one story portico and into a large reception room. To each side of this was a parlor of equal size. These three rooms were very large and well decorated. The ceilings were frescoed about 1850 by journeymen artists and were exceptionally fine. One of these still remains. The west wing consisted of a large dining room and pantry. There was a summer kitchen outside with living quarters and a dairy. The winter kitchen and slave quarters were in the basement. It is a large, full basement that repeats the floor plan above it. Access to the basement is only from the outside. All windows are original. In the front they are four over six panes and nine over six in the rest of the house. The roof is original tin shingles.

One remaining fresco.

The house was built for gracious living and was the scene of much social activity. When this house passed out of the Yancey family, it was first privately owned and extensive modernization was done. It was then purchased commercially for the land and the house was neglected for many years. Now it is privately owned. With the help of the Yancey family members who have provided the owners with photos and stories, the new owners are undertaking renovations.

SILAM SELLARS

c. 1800

In 1781, Michael Sellars received the deed to this large tract of land. The deed was signed by Thomas Jefferson, then the Governor of Virginia.[1] Michael Sellars was a soldier in the Revolutionary War. His son, Andrew built the first part of this log house. Construction was completed by his son, Silam around 1859 as a T shaped extension.

Since the Sellars were spiritual leaders in the community, they let circuit riders hold services in their home. In 1788 a log structure called the Sellars Chapel was built on their land. Six years later a

---

[1] Virginia had an entail system until 1776. This system restricted inheritance to owners lineal descendants, in particular, to his male children. At this time, only people who owned land could vote. Jefferson outlawed the entail system to enable more people to vote. Also, more settlement was encouraged in the western part of Virginia.

Funeral door before renovation.

school was built. Andrew Sellars also deeded a church site that was to become Fellowship Methodist Church. An 1899 deed shows evidence of other houses and structures on the property as the family evolved.

The original house is all that stands today. The first floor of this log house is a hall and parlor plan. It is divided into two rooms, the larger one containing the front entrance. An open staircase is on the rear wall of this room and a door leading to the basement is on another wall. The other small room has an interesting door that opens to the outside. This is an oversized door that has been identified as a funeral door. The size allowed easy movement of caskets in and out of the house. The door sill is at wagon height and does not have a loading platform or stoop. A funeral door was usually seen in Northern homes. Both rooms on the first floor have fireplaces with elaborate carved mantels. The stairs now land in a hall. There are enclosed stairs that lead to a trap door for the attic. Originally, there was one large room upstairs. It is now divided into two rooms. Both rooms have fireplaces with plain mantels. In the attic, exposed wooden pegged beams support the gabled roof. The roof is original tin. The foundation is made of cut stone with a small cellar on the west side. There is an original hand dug well nearby that has been restored.

When the current owners purchased this house, the house was in poor condition. When the vinyl siding was removed to reveal logs, it was decided to restore and renovate this home. The T extension was replaced. Extensive repair work was done inside and out to return this home to its original condition. It is a private residence.

1967 photo by Isaac L. Terrell.

Old Houses in Rockingham County Revisited

SITES HOUSE
c. 1800

Also known as the Ben Kline place, this is one of the two German style, central chimney stone houses existing in Rockingham County. The exterior of this house is similar to Mannheim.

The exact date is difficult to determine but this property was first owned by the Sites family. The original house was of logs and the stone house was erected in front of it. This was either done by John Sites or his son, George. It then became a farm house with the usual dependencies in the surrounding area.

David B. Kline bought the house in 1891. The log section was then torn down and a frame addition was erected in its place. The house then was sold to William Henry Caricofe in the 1870's who lived there only a few years. In 1883, the house became the property of Ben Kline and remained in the Kline family until it was sold at public auction in 1976. The current owners bought this house in 1988.

This house is a three over two plan. The chimney is slightly off center. Two large rooms on the first floor run the depth of the house.

To the right of the front door, as one enters the house, is a small boxed stairway which ascends to the second floor which contains one large room to the north and two rooms to the south.

The doors, interior window casing and floors are of yellow pine. Exterior walls are eighteen inches thick and interior dividing walls are vertical pine boards joined together in a tongue and groove style. Interior plaster is original and there is the original whitewash upstairs. Most hardware is original. There is a half cellar with a wet weather spring.

When the current owners purchased this house in 1988, it had been empty since 1952. It had no modern conveniences and very few changes had been made over the years. A four year restoration project was begun. The 1870 frame addition was restored and a sympathetic addition was added to accommodate modern conveniences. Much of the original material was saved and repaired. During restoration, the name of the stone mason, J. M. Bulh, was discovered in the cellar, but there is no date. Also the name of Dorcas Lee Harrison-1845 appears on the wall of the second floor west room. Her identity so far is a mystery to the owners.

Old Houses in Rockingham County Revisited

Although this house was unoccupied for over thirty years, it was in a remarkable state of preservation when the current owners purchased it. With the restoration complete, this house provides a testimony to the excellent building skills of early county settlers.

VLR; NRHP

Undated photographs of the Sites House. The people are Kline family members.

Tunker House
c. 1800

The term "tunker" originates from the German work "tunken" meaning to immerse. The early Brethren Church, which originated in Germany and spread into the Shenandoah Valley, based its beliefs around the principle of baptism by trine or triple immersion. The members were at one time called Dunkers or Dunkards.

The original portion of this house, now known as The Tunker House was built in 1794 by Rudolph Yount. He was born in Switzerland and came to America in 1749, settling first in York, Pennsylvania. There he helped found the Codorus Congregation Church of York County. In 1794 he came to Broadway, Virginia where his two sons, Benjamin and Jacob Yount, had purchased 300 acres of land.

This Flemish bond brick house is a four over four plan. Every room, with one exception, has a fireplace, two of them are corner design. There is also a fireplace in the basement. There is a tin roof and the windows are original. Most of the floors are twelve-inch-wide pine

boards. Some of the doors are six paneled. The doors and cabinets have authentic hardware.

The central portion of the house, which was built in 1802, provided a double living room area, eighteen by thirty five feet in dimension. It was divided by large wooden panels that were hinged to swung up to the ceiling on large iron hinges. It was here that the Dunkards or more properly the Society of Tunkers, an early name for the Brethren Church, held services. The house and tannery was inherited by Elizabeth Yount, who was married to the Reverend Peter Nead of Hagerstown, Maryland. He was the author of *Primitive Christianity*. This was the Brethren's first theological work published in English. In 1839 the farm passed into the hands of Mrs. Nead's brother, Samuel Yount and then changed hands

This photo shows Flemish bond brick on the house and American common bond on the chimney, which is not key into the house. The chimney was probably rebuilt and the iron rod added at a later date.

three times until it became the property of Abraham and Samuel Shank in 1868. Then it was sold to Mr. John Zigler. It remained in the Zigler family for almost a century.

The house was restored by Reverend and Mrs. S. D. Lindsay, a Church of the Brethren minister. It is now owned by a member of the family and is in excellent condition.

VLR; NRHP

Unique swinging wooden panels.

JOHN BEERY HOUSE
1803

This is the first house built on the Beery homestead. (see John K. Beery House) Abraham Beery immigrated into Rockingham County about 1770 and purchased large land holdings along Linville Creek. He was originally from Switzerland, coming to America through Holland. He was a Mennonite. His son, John, built this house in 1803. He also built a mill with carding machines that made blankets and wove cloth. The mill was frame and burned around 1810-1812.

This house is a "T" shaped, two story brick house, facing away from the creek. It is possible that the extension to the west was perhaps the original house. This contained one large room with loft, a large fireplace, and covered a full basement which had a large fireplace. A beehive shaped bake oven was originally attached to this chimney, but has been removed.

The main portion of the house was divided by interior walls of tongue and groove pine boards. The first floor had three rooms with an enclosed circular staircase going to the attic. The second floor was divided into four rooms that connected because there were no hallways in the house. There were only two fireplaces in this portion of the house, one in the large room on the south side and one in one of the rooms on the north side. The windows in this house are not original.[1]

The interior of this house has been renovated because of a fire. However, the exterior remains intact and is in good condition.

Undated photos. Note the end chimneys.

---

[1] United States Government, "Works Progress Administration Historical American Buildings Survey, Rockingham County, 1935-1939," Virginia State Library, Richmond, Virginia, Photographic Files, unbound, uncataloged.

Old Houses in Rockingham County Revisited

JOSEPH FUNK HOUSE
1804

Joseph Funk was born in Berks County, Pennsylvania in 1777, the son of Henry and Barbara Showalter Funk. In 1786 his parents moved to Rockingham County and settled on a tract of land near Sparkling Springs. In 1804 he married Elizabeth Rhodes and they built this house in what was then the beginning of the town of Singers Glen.

Joseph Funk specialized in the study of music and became an authority in sacred song. He was influential in the evolution of the patent note system of musical notation, and his book, the famous *Harmonica Sacra*, has gone through twenty editions.

He was a member of the Mennonite Church, which has always emphasized the importance of sacred song. In addition to his publishing business he found time to organize and teach vocal music classes in many counties of Virginia and adjoining states.[1]

---

[1] John W. Wayland, *Historic Homes of Northern Virginia*, Staunton, Virginia, The McClure Company, Inc., 1937, p. 203.

This house is one and one-half stories high with a one story addition to the rear. It is log with weather boards. There is one end chimney and dormer windows on the second story. The interior was modernized in 1934 and the entire house is in excellent condition.

It is maintained as a private residence.

VLR; NRHP

Exterior shot taken by John Wayland around 1932; courtesy of Bridgewater College, Bridgewater, Virginia.

Opposite page, top right: Interior shot taken by John Wayland in 1932; courtesy of Bridgewater College, Bridgewater, Virginia.

Opposite page, bottom right: Photo taken in 1911 from John Wayland's collection of photographs. Joseph Funk's grandson and his wife are in the photo. In right foreground is the old log loom house that was converted into the print shop in 1847; courtesy Handley Library, Winchester, Virginia.

Old Houses in Rockingham County Revisited

BRENNEMAN HOUSE
1804

Abraham Brenneman (1744-1815) was born in Lancaster, Pennsylvania and migrated to Rockingham County in 1775. Here he became a prominent farmer and land owner. He was a member of the Mennonite faith and donated land for the Lindale Mennonite Church.

The main portion of the house is rectangular plan, with ten rooms and seven fireplaces. It was built of brick which were made on the premises. The brick has been covered with stucco. There is unusual decorative cornice and eve trim work. One very interesting feature of this house is the fact that it was built with two kitchen wings. The reason for this is not known, but both rooms are large in size, and both have large fireplaces and are built over a cellar.

There is a center hallway with open staircase leading to the attic. Partitioning inside walls are tongue and groove boards, and some of the original doors and hardware survive. There is another small enclosed stairway leading from the north kitchen to a loft which was used for storage.[1]

---

[1] United States Government, Works Progress Administration, "Historical

This house is a private residence and it is in good condition. The current owners plan to continue preservation of this home.

footnote 1 continued

American Buildings Survey, Rockingham, County, 1935-1939," Virginia State Library, Richmond, Virginia, Photographic Files, unbound, uncataloged.

93

1750 to 1850

Sipe-Davis
1811

This house is referred to as "The Stone House," "The Colonel Sipe House" or the "Davis House". It was built in 1811 by Christian Kratzer II on an estate of 4000 acres inherited from his father, Christian Kratzer, who came to America with his family from Germany. It was built as a barn, one of three which existed on the Kratzer farm. (see Kratzer House) Two were destroyed during the Civil War.

This house is built of limestone, with walls more than two feet thick, and contains twenty-one rooms. It was converted into a dwelling shortly after the Civil War. At this time it was occupied by the late Colonel Emanuel Sipe and Mrs. Sipe, who was a granddaughter of Mr. Kratzer. For a number of years, Mr. Sipe conducted a general merchandise store on the ground floor with his residence on the two floors above.[1]

---

[1] United States Government, Works Progress Administration, "Historical American Buildings Survey, Rockingham County, 1935-1939," Virginia State Library, Richmond, Virginia.

Old Houses in Rockingham County Revisited

In 1896 or 1897, Mr. Ritz, a German, operated a cheese factory in this house. Evidence of the cooling troughs may still be seen. Later it was the home of Turner Ashby Rhinehart, a great grandson of Mr. Kratzer. During this time it housed the Linville Post Office. In 1909, it was purchased by Mr. and Mrs. Isaac Davis, who converted the ground floor into two apartments and lived on the two top floors.

It is now privately owned and has been converted into an apartment house. It is in a good state of repair.

BOWMAN SELLERS HOUSE
1816

This is a fine English type, "L" shaped brick house overlooking the banks of Smith's Creek. It is two stories high with a stone foundation. There is a chimney on each end and a front porch with four square columns. The bricks are laid in Flemish bond, and the nine over nine windows are original. Inside there are eight large rooms. A wide center hall has a staircase leading three flights to an attic. There is also an enclosed staircase leading from the kitchen to the second floor.

All interior walls are solid brick, which have been plastered. There is a chair rail in all rooms, with wide pine molding around the doors and windows. Each room on the first floor has a fireplace with a mantel. The second floor has three fireplaces with small mantels. The cellar has a flagstone floor and the brick walls are thirteen inches thick.

Miller Bowman (1750-1832) settled on Smith's Creek and married Phoebe Harrison, daughter of John Harrison. It is thought that he built this house, now known as the Sellers place, about 1816. The land on which it was built dates back to Zebulon Harrison who owned a large amount of property in this area. The Bowman family united in marriage with the Sellers family in 1854 and this house has remained in this family since that date.

This home is a private residence and in excellent condition.

Peter Acker House
1818

Of the brick houses built in the county during the early part of the nineteenth century this house, known as the Peter Acker house, is outstanding in design, construction and site. Located on Linville Creek, it was built in 1818 of locally fired brick laid in Flemish bond on all four sides. Usually Flemish bond was displayed on the front of

the house, while the remaining three sides were laid in common bond. The name of Andrew Brown, with the date, was inscribed in stone on a gabled end. His identity remains a mystery, and it is hard to determine whether he was the master builder or one of the workmen.

Originally, it was an "L" shaped house with an extension to the east, but this has

Inscription of Andrew Brown on the north gable end.

been removed leaving it a five room house with cellar and attic. The first floor is divided into three rooms with center hallway. The hall is created with one wall of solid brick and one of vertical pine boards. The large room on the north side has a beautiful carved mantel with medallions and reeding. From this room ascends a small boxed staircase. The step ends in this room are exceptionally fine and rare in houses of this area.

Mantel with reedings and medallions design.

Step ends with scroll work.

The south side is divided into two rooms. Each has a corner fireplace. The mantels are also hand carved. Another small boxed staircase ascends from the room on the southwest. Originally there was no doorway between the two rooms on the second floor.

An unusual feature of this house is the fort cellar which exists under the south section. This large room has an arched ceiling and slotted window. Fort cellars are not uncommon in Rockingham County although the reason for their construction at this date is purely speculative as the threat of Indian attacks was over. It is locally assumed that the existing house was built over the foundation of an earlier structure which was built for defense. There is a spring house behind this house. Inside this spring house is a large iron kettle that could hold up to one hundred forty gallons. One theory is that nitrate was cooked in it to make gunpowder during the Civil War.

Peter Acker, sometimes spelled Aucker, was a large land holder on

Linville Creek. In 1806 he was known to have holdings of 654 acres. His property joined the Lincoln Homestead. He and his wife are buried in Old Breneman's Cemetery.

This house is a private residence and in excellent condition.

Inside the fort cellar.

Photo taken in the 1950's of two Acker family members; courtesy Margie Nafzinger.

BARBEE HOUSE
1818

This imposing house is an "L" shaped two story house constructed of handmade brick. It is enhanced by a double porch across the front supported by four Doric columns. It has a metal gable roof. It has a two story porch and a second floor balustrade.

First used as a tavern it was known as "Barbee's Tavern" prior to the Civil War. It is reported that Henry Clay and Andrew Jackson slept here.[1] Following the Civil War it was used as a school for young ladies operated by Colonel Barbee's daughters, Mollie Barbee and her sister Mrs. Gabriel Terrell.

Colonel Gabriel Barbee, undated photo; courtesy The Virginia Historical Society, Richmond, Virginia.

---

[1] United States Government, "Works Progress Administration, Historical American Buildings Survey, Rockingham County, 1935-1939," Virginia State Library, Richmond, Virginia.

The house takes it name from Colonel Gabriel Barbee. Born in 1825 in what is now Panorama, on top of the pass in Thornton's Gap, Blue Ridge, he was one of twelve children. Settling in Bridgewater at the end of the Civil War, he bought this house and one acre of land from R.N. Poole for $1500.00. [2] His brother, William Randolph (1818-1868) and William's son, Herbert (1848-1936) were both sculptors. The "Colonel" was a skilled wood carver and his specialty was intricately decorated canes that he gave to his friends.[3] He lived in Bridgewater for many years and was mayor of the town. He died September 4, 1908.

The original house was two rooms over two with a one story ell extension to the west. There was a courtyard behind the original house next to the ell. This was the maids quarters and had a staircase to the second floor rooms. The center hallway has a walnut staircase. In the first floor south room is a wall mural, now covered, as well as ceiling frescoes reflecting its formal use. The north room was used as a sitting room.

Above: Walnut staircase.
Right: Wall mural.

[2] May, C.E, *Life Under 4 Flags*, McClure Publishing, Verona, Virginia, 1982. p. 447.

[3] Wayland, John, *Men of Mark and Representative-Citizens of Harrisonburg and Rockingham County*, McClure Company, Staunton, Virginia, p. 389.

Some of the floors are original and each room has a fireplace with mantel. All windows and doors are original. The doors still have the original brass numbers from the tavern days. A large addition was added during the mid to late 19th century which enclosed in the courtyard and added two large rooms on the second floor with a center hallway. The original corbelled brick cornices are still in evidence.

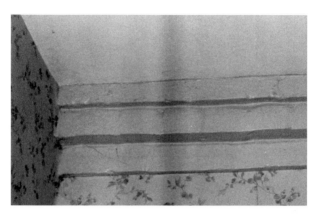

Corbelled brick.

Later, a two story brick wing was built to the south end of the ell to make a main floor kitchen and pantry. So, now the front hallway on the second floor runs the entire depth of the house. Four bedrooms, two on each side are in the back portion of the house with two rooms and a bathroom on the front block. There is a large unfinished basement, with three rooms, which is below the original part of the house.

There is no information available on the original owners of the Barbee House. R.N. and Mary Pool and Gabriel T. Barbee bought it in 1867. Colonel Barbee operated an inn in the late 19th century. When he died, the house exchanged hand several times until 1922, when William Homan, Sr. bought the house and remodeled it into a single family dwelling. In 1944, the house was purchased by the family of the current owners.

Now a private residence, this house is in an excellent state of preservation.

VLR; NRHP

INGLEWOOD
1818

Although this is one of the loveliest of all the houses built in Rockingham County, very little can be determined about its history. The land on which it was built was granted to either Michael Bowyer or Thomas Ewing in 1742. In 1818 it was purchased by Robert Gray, a prominent attorney. It is felt that he built the house for his son Douglas on the occasion of his marriage to Isabella Pickney, daughter of the diplomat William Pickney.

The selection of the site for this house is evidence that it was made by one with an appreciation of the beauty of its natural site. It is situated on top of a hill which commands an imposing view for many miles around it. This property adjoins Belle Grove.

The house itself was skillfully designed and enhances its natural setting. It is built of brick, English style, with double chimneys and a service extension on the east side. There is a gable roof with a regular five bay face. There is a full complement of outbuildings and farm buildings surrounding the house. Throughout its history, "Inglewood" has been renowned for its gracious living and was the scene of many and varied social activities.

It became the property of General John E. Roller in 1876. General Roller was a prominent Harrisonburg attorney. He was a lieutenant of scouts and engineers during the Civil War. He was appointed major-general of the Virginia militia in 1872. He died in 1918. The current owner purchased the estate from his daughter in 1945.

This home is privately owned and in good condition

VLR; NRHP

J. Owen Beard House
1819

This brick house was built in two sections. The original house, built in 1819 by Joseph Wenger on land purchased from Joseph Linville, was a bank house with two stories and a loft which faced north.

The first floor or basement was used as a cooking and eating room. A spring flowed through this room, and a portion of it is still exposed. The basement was divided into two rooms: a dairy and food storage room with outside door, and the other, with a large fireplace and mantel, used for cooking and eating.

The second floor was divided into two rooms of equal size. The smaller room over the dairy has a small fireplace on the north side, which was not in the original house, and a small enclosed stairway ascended to the second floor. The larger room has a large fireplace, which is original, on the west side and an outside door opening onto ground level.

In 1835 a new house was built adjacent to the old house. It was a rectangular structure running north and south, with plans that the old one would be torn down. Instead, the two houses were joined together, the roof of the old house being raised to a full two stories, thus completing the present building.

The space between the two houses, which is approximately three feet wide, was enclosed in brick, leaving a void between. It is alleged that during the Civil War valuables were lowered on ropes through a loose board in the attic and hung in this space for safe keeping.

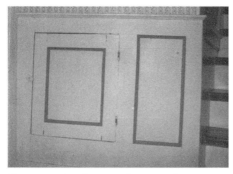

Door covering the space between the two houses.

The house is made of handmade brick and retains the original tin roof. It has undergone some remodeling and reconstruction but much of the original woodwork, floors, doors and windows remain. At one time there were three enclosed staircases in this house, but these have been removed, and the house is served from a center hall and stairway.

There are ten rooms in the house, including the entrance hall and the basement rooms, which are now used for storage. The only remaining outbuilding is the loom house, which has been converted into a dwelling. A distinctive feature of this house are the circular brick columns.

This house is a private residence. A descendent of J. Owen Beard and her family maintain this house as a private residence. It is in excellent condition.

Round brick columns on the rear porch.

Linville Edom Home Demonstration Club, 1920-1930. Club members are sitting on the front steps on this house; photo courtesy of Mrs. Karal Atchison, granddaughter of Mamie Terrell. Front row: Pearl Rhodes (Artista), Mae Wenger (I.L.), Willie Frances Myers (Ike F.), Mamie Davis Terrell (C.N.), Sadie Fries Barrick (Raymond) Back row: Mary Kratzer Simmers (John), Pauline Fawley Beard (J.O.), Bess Shaver Pugh (Bob) Demonstrators- Carrie Bowman, Willie Myers Miller.

Undated photo of Beard family members on the east side of the house.

JOHN K BEERY
1819

This stone house was once a prosperous homestead. The Beerys sold the property in 1920, at which time it became a rental property until the 1940's. It was abandoned until the current owners purchased it in 1975. It has been carefully restored and is once again a beautiful home. This was the second Beery house built on the Beery homestead. It was a complete setting with a spring house, wash house, servants' house, a carriage stepping stone and a large limestone barn with slotted ends.

John A. Beery gave this wooded plot of land to his son John K. Beery. (see John Beery House) He was nineteen and getting married. The original house was built in 1819 and had two rooms with a shingled roof. John and his wife had fifteen children. A two story addition was built in

Isaac Beery

1750 to 1850

1835-36. Large folding doors divide the original two rooms. Beery was a strict Mennonite who held services in his home as he was opposed to the use of churches. The new addition added another fireplace and access to a small cellar. In 1835, a cook and wash house was also built near Buttermilk Creek.

John's first son, Isaac N., stayed to help with the farm. Isaac and his wife had ten children. He remained here until his death in 1920. In 1839, another addition was built to the west end of the house which consisted of two rooms over two. The interior stone walls are plastered. All dividing walls are tongue and grooved upright boards in the main rooms. There are fireplaces with mantels in the main rooms and built in cupboards on the sides. Each room has a painted chair rail.

Also in 1835, work was begun on the stone barn. On the high west peak of the barn is the name Fesler for David Fesler (Feshler), the stone mason, and the date 1839. The slots are for ventilation. It was not a fort barn since the last Indian raid was 1805.

Barn with ventilation slots.

The barn was burned during the Civil War. The end walls stood and the barn was repaired with a frame south wall. Before the war there was a frame tenant house near the cook and wash house. Also, the loom house was built in 1839 north of the main house. After the war, the ice house was built. The well house was built in 1866 with a trough for diary products.

All restoration and history of this house has been well documented. The owners allow the Beery families to hold reunions on the property.

VLS; NRHP

Isaac Beery and son showing off their horses for sale.

1932 photograph taken by the Historic American Buildings Survey; courtesy of the Library of Virginia, Richmond, Virginia.

ELDER JOHN KLINE HOUSE
1820

John Kline, born in 1797, was an active leader among the Brethren in the middle of the 19th century. Largely by his own efforts he became a farmer, evangelist, physician, traveler, author, philanthropist, church leader and, finally, Christian martyr. He was called to the ministry in 1834 and devoted thirty years of his life to this call.

After the outbreak of the Civil War, Elder Kline was an ardent worker for peace and understanding. He was influential in having the Exemption Act for conscientious objectors passed by the Virginia Assembly. With the passing of the Exemption Act of 1862 by the Confederate States, men had to prove membership in the Brethren or Mennonite Church before Virginia's succession from the Union. Since these people were pacifists, they were fined before the war for not showing up at militia role calls.[1] Elder John Kline secured the release

---

[1] Heatwole, John, *The Burning, Sheridan in the Shenandoah Valley*, Charlottesville, Virginia, Howell Press, Inc., 1998, p. 59.

Old Houses in Rockingham County Revisited

of all those drafted from his congregation, providing much of the redemption money from his own pocket. In 1864, the law was stricken as the Confederate States needed soldiers.

During the four years of the war, he had been given permits to go and come freely through both the Northern and Southern army lines because he was fully trusted by both civil and military authorities. Local gossip, however accused him of bearing military secrets to Federal generals but there was never any evidence. But on June 15, 1864 while riding west of his home, he was shot and killed by Southern sympathizers.

In 1830, Elder John Kline gave the land upon which the Linville Creek Church of the Brethren was built. Prior to this date, meetings were held in his house. The house stands near the Tunker House, which was also used as a meeting house for the early Church of the Brethren.

It is a substantial brick house built in the same style as many other brick houses of this period. The main part of the house, facing east, was actually one large room with hinged partitions dividing it into two rooms and a center hall. These walls are now stationary but the hooks which held them to the ceiling can still be seen. There is one large chimney on the south end which supplied a large fireplace for his audience room. The brick in this house is laid in Flemish bond, and some of the locks and hinges are original.

The house is privately owned and in excellent condition.

LOCUST GROVE
1820

One of the most beautifully located old homes in Rockingham County is "Locust Grove". It is built on high ground in a slight valley and is surrounded by cedars and a few giant locust trees.

The house, which now takes the shape of a large square with a back ell, is the product of several remodelings and renovations. The original part of this house, which is the north side, was built of logs in 1820 and is a four room two story structure, larger than most houses of that period.

Most log houses built in Rockingham County in the 18th century are of the pioneer type with end chimneys. The log portion of "Locust Grove" was constructed with a center chimney placed to the back of the house allowing corner fireplaces to be built on both floors.

The house was built by Daniel Mathews, the son of Solomon Mathews, a Pennsylvania Quaker, who migrated to Rockingham County before the Revolutionary War. He was a land owner and a worker of iron. He owned an iron furnace on Linville Creek, called

"Mount Ert" as well as land on Smith's Creek, near Lacey Springs, where he operated a furnace known as "Spring Forge."

Daniel Mathews (1779-1842) was a farmer and public servant. His daughter, Hannah, married Hiram Martz and "Locust Grove" came into the possession of the Martz family where it remained until recent years.[1]

The Martz family undertook two renovations. The first renovation turned the four room log house into an eight room house. On the south side, two large outside chimneys were built to furnish fireplaces for the four new rooms. New double windows were placed across the front as well as a large flat topped porch.

"Locust Grove" was always the scene of gracious living, and it was to strengthen this reputation that the house was again enlarged in the 1900's. A large dining room was built onto the west side of the house with the upper floor providing two more bedrooms. This, plus a new kitchen, brought the total number of rooms in the house to twelve.

The Martz sisters maintained "Locust Grove" as a tourist home during the 1920's-1930's dispensing good food and gracious living to their guests.

This house is in ruins.

Photo taken in 1932 by the Historic American Buildings Survey; courtesy the Library of Virginia, Richmond, Virginia.

---

[1] Houston Harrison, *Settlers of the Long Grey Trail*, Dayton, Virginia, Joseph K. Ruebush-Elkins Co., 1935, p.336.

EMANUEL ROLLER HOUSE
1820

This large heavy timber frame house, now known as the Emanuel Roller house, is built on land which was a part of an original patent land grant on Cook's Creek, issued to the Kiser family in approximately 1790. The Kisers owned most of the land which lies on the west side of Route 11 from the town of Mount Crawford north to the Pleasant Valley road. This house was first owned by the Irck family, then by the Henebergers, the Arians, the Perrys and then came into the ownership of the Roller family.

When the Valley Turnpike was traversed by stagecoaches, this house was used as a stage stop and tavern. The house is well proportioned with large chimneys at either end, partially exposed on the exterior. The chimney on the west side is of stone and common bond brick. The one on the east side is of brick laid in Flemish bond. The windows in this house are original. They are mostly three paned but some are four paned, which is unique for this vintage house.

Old Houses in Rockingham County Revisited

The interior of the house is divided into three rooms on the first floor and three second floor rooms with a center hall and open staircase. There are two exterior doors on the north side, one original and one added later. There is a basement under the house, opening onto the lower or south side. These basement rooms served as cooking and food storage areas. There is a huge attic that probably was used as a sleeping area for tavern customers and travelers.

This house has stood empty for many years and is uninhabitable.

THE MORRISON HOUSE
1820-1824

The land on which this house stood was conveyed on November 20, 1781 by Thomas Harrison and wife, Sarah, to Dr. Samuel Gay. Dr. Gay had been a surgeon in one of Muehlenbergs regiments during the Revolutionary War. It is probably that Dr. Gay erected a house on his lot soon thereafter. The previous year, 1780, he was issued a license to keep a tavern in the town. In 1791, records show that he was the town jailer. It was not unusual for the local tavern to serve as the local jail.

On May 12, 1810, Dr. Gay and his wife, Catherine, sold their house to Henry McArey. On October 8, 1819, Adam Fisher and his wife sold the same lot with dwelling to Joseph Thornton. A map with the description of the prison bounds show a house on the same corner, and the accompanying description designates as "Thorntons Brick House." At that time the brick extension on the west side was not shown. It can only be concluded that the main portion of the house was built by Joseph Thornton between 1820 and 1824.[1]

---

[1] John W. Wayland, *Historic Harrisonburg*, Staunton, Virginia, The McClure Printing Company, 1949, p.128.

Old Houses in Rockingham County Revisited

The Morrison family moved into this house in 1858, renting it first from Andrew Irck. Records are not clear, but it could be assumed that Mr. Irck built the extension on the west side. The Morrison family later purchased the house and lived there until the death of Miss Elizabeth Morrison in 1968. Mr. Morrison was a carriage maker, and his shop was located in the frame building which stood next door.

This house was built of brick, laid in Flemish bond. There were four rooms; two on the first floor and two on the second floor. These were served by a center hall and open staircase which continued to the attic. All four rooms had fireplaces and mantels. The windows were nine panes over six on both floors.

The brick extension on the west side was originally one long room on the first floor with two rooms on the second. This portion has served many purposes. It was used as a post office in 1854 and later used as a tavern. It was also partitioned off into two brick rooms serving as kitchen and dining room. Originally, the kitchen was housed in a separate brick building which stood adjacent to the main house.

This house was torn down and the property is used commercially.

THE GROVE
1822

This large brick house was the home place of the Ewing family. The founding ancestor of this family, William Ewing, was born in Scotland and came to America in 1718, landing in Philadelphia and then settling in Bucks County, Pennsylvania.

He came to the Valley of Virginia in 1742 and made his first land purchase of 200 acres on which he built his home. Why it was called "The Grove" is not known. The first house was of logs. The present brick house was built in 1822 by William Ewing, II (1780-1850) .[1] William Ewing II was closely identified with affairs of the county. He was a successful farmer, owning a large plantation of excellent land. This house remained in the Ewing family for one hundred and seventy seven years.

This house has a center hall with one large room to the right and

---

[1] Houston Harrison, *Settlers by the Long Grey Trail*, Dayton, Virginia, The Ruebush-Elkins Co., 1935, p.447.

Left: Carved mantel Right: Half round columns on the east side of the house.

two rooms to the left. In the large room is an elaborate carved mantel. There is a tight boxed staircase toward the rear of the hall which ascends to the second floor and on to the attic. Upstairs there are four rooms. There is an addition to the side of the house which now has a large room with an apartment above. Every room has a fireplace with a different mantel. All the floors, doors and hardware are original. The doors are six paneled. The original two-column, double portico has been replaced with a more modern porch running the full length of the house. Other slight changes have been made to the house.

This is a private residence and is in excellent condition.

1932 photo taken by the Historic American Buildings Survey; note the second floor door.

121

Hiram Kite House
1822

The Kite family came to Rockingham County from Orange County around the end of the eighteenth century. William Kite was the first Kite to settle in the Elkton area. His land grant was signed by Governor Monroe in 1801 and extended from the top of the Blue Ridge Mountains to the banks of the Shenandoah.

William Kite built this house around 1822. The brick was made on the premises and is laid in Flemish bond. He married Anna Elizabeth Harnsberger, daughter of Conrad Harnsberger. They had nine children. In 1843, after the deaths of William and his wife, two of their

Hiram Kite (courtesy of Miss Kite)

sons, Conrad and Hiram, bought this house from the other children. It remained the home of Hiram Kite for the rest of his life. He married Margaret Miller, great, great granddaughter of Adam Miller. (see Adam Miller House) Captain Kite was a captain in the Civil War, serving in Company H, 2nd Regiment of the 7th Brigade Virginia Militia. After the war, Elk Lithia Spring was developed by him. This water is reputed to have great medicinal values and evidence of the original spring house and spring still exist behind this house. He also owned the William Kite House. He lived to be eighty nine years old.

This brick and frame house is in an "L" shape. The ell extension now has vinyl siding covering the original wood. There are three chimneys, one on each end and one in the rear. There are eight rooms in the house but only seven fireplaces. All the mantels are different. The chimney in the rear of the house does not serve a room on the second floor. This house has two stairways. In the front hall is an open staircase that ascends to the attic. An enclosed staircase ascends from the dining room to the second floor. An unusual feature of this house was two unusually wide doors. One is at the end of the front hall and another one was in the first floor west wing. Later renovations made

Photograph taken in 1932 by the Historical American Buildings Survey; courtesy of the Library of Virginia.

this one smaller. Both doors would have opened onto the back porch. It is likely that they were funeral doors.

A single porch, which is not original, runs the entire front of the house. The columns are in the plain box style and there is a transom entrance. There was a double porch on the rear which is now gone. The interior doors are heavy six paneled. The floor is original and made of six inch boards. There is a half basement with a fireplace and a full attic. The current tin roof replaced the original slate shingle roof.

This home is a private residence and is undergoing renovations.

VLR

Jacob Lincoln Jr. House
Lincoln Hall
Lincoln-Pennybacker House
1825

This house was built by the third son and eighth child of Captain Jacob Lincoln. It stands near the site of the Bryan homestead. In 1744 O'Bryans, (later Bryans) erected a cabin probably near the spring house on the original 600 acres of land. The road on which this house fronts is the Old Indian Trail stretching from the Shenandoah Valley to Ohio. George Washington passed here on September 30, 1784. In 1767, John Lincoln, great grandfather of the President, came to Linville Creek and bought land about one mile north of this house. Around 1800, John Lincolns' son, Jacob Sr. built the Lincoln Homestead which is south of this property.

Jacob's son, Jacob Jr. built the brick part of Lincoln Hall. He mar-

125

ried a widow with two children. They had nine more children. In 1840, she went insane and spent the last twenty-six years of her life in what is now Western State Hospital. Jacob died in 1848 in Ohio.

Dr. Richard Maupin, who married Jacobs' niece, Mary Elizabeth Lincoln, was appointed guardian of the children. As each child became of age, the Maupins bought out their land inheritance. Dr. Maupin died in 1855 leaving his widow and three children. In 1865, Elizabeth married J.D. Pennybacker and had three more children. In 1874, Elizabeth's mother died. She inherited the Lincoln Homestead which was sold to settle the estate. With this money, Elizabeth tore down half of the house. A frame addition and front porch was added to the brick section [1] Elizabeth's daughter, Kate, inherited the house full of Lincoln furniture. She spent her entire life in this house until her death in 1938. After passing through several other hands, the current owners purchased this house in 1988.

This house has received many famous visitors. Dr. John Wayland, a local historian, brought several authors to the house to do research on the Lincolns. They included Carl Sandberg, Ida Tarbell, who wrote a biography of the Lincolns and Hamlin Garland. Abraham Lincoln's son, Robert Todd, visited there in 1903.

Original pine shingles as seen from the attic.

---

[1] John W. Wayland, *The Lincolns in Virginia*, Staunton, Virginia, The McClure Company, Inc., 1937, p.165.

Faux painted mantel.

The house still has the original white pine shingles. They are preserved beneath a metal roof that Kate Pennybacker added. The exterior of the house indicates that the well to do Lincolns were interested in appearance. Symmetry of the house is made possible by a false chimney.

One enters the front door and there is a large main hall with a wide staircase leading to the second floor. To the left are two rooms with brick interior walls and fireplaces. The mantels are painted with a faux wood grain. To the right of the main hall are the rooms in the frame section of the house. A parlor in the front room has a rare black marble mantel. A door leads to the dining room and kitchen. From the kitchen there are steps that lead to the original servants quarters upstairs. There is no access to the rest of the house from these rooms. Four large bedrooms are on the second floor. Ceilings are nine feet high. The basement is under the original brick part of the house and it

Black marble mantel.

was originally the kitchen and cooks quarters.

This house is a private residence. The current owners have done extensive renovations and have done much research into the past of this historical home.

Photo taken by John Wayland of Lincoln Hall in 1932; courtesy Handley Library, Winchester, Virginia.

Old Houses in Rockingham County Revisited

HOMELAND
KYLE MEADOWS
1825

This property was acquired from Robert Cravens, whose father, John, received the land by grant in 1755. The original grant included five thousand acres.[1] This farm was a gift from Jeremiah Kyle to his son, Robert Kyle. Jeremiah's father, David Kyle, was born in 1757 in Northern Ireland. David came to the Valley as a peddler. Upon his death in 1844, David Kyle was reported to be one of the wealthiest men in Rockingham County. He became a merchant and owned a farm of 760 acres. Jeremiah Kyle was also a merchant. He operated a general merchandise store on Court Square in Harrisonburg. He was also a farmer.

Robert Kyle married Mary Byrd, whose father was Abraham Byrd of "Red Banks," near Craney Island. [2] The Byrds moved to "Stoneleigh

---

[1] United States Government, Works Progress Administration, "Historical American Buildings Survey, Rockingham County, 1935-1939," Bridgewater College microfilm.

[2] United States Government, Works Progress Administration, "Historical American Buildings Survey, Rockingham County, 1935-1939," Bridgewater College microfilm.

Inn" in Harrisonburg at an undetermined date. After Robert's death, Mary married Reverend Lemuel Seeton Reed in 1867. He was the father of Dr. Walter Reed. They lived in Charlottesville until 1869 when they returned home to care for Mrs. Byrd. The Reeds owned this house until 1877. Walter Reed did visit Harrisonburg on several occasions.[3]

After changing hands several times, the house was sold in 1950 to a family that made the south addition. First Presbyterian Church bought the property in 1960. In 1963 a new congregation was organized. The house was then remodeled to create a sanctuary, church rooms, pastor's study, and kitchen to serve the needs of the congregation and community.

Homeland is a large two story brick house. There are four Doric columns below a portico. It is beautifully sited on a large sloping lawn. There is a center hall with a staircase. The original house had eight rooms with fireplaces and mantels.[4]

Even though this house has not retained much of its original interior features, it has an important history. It is well maintained as a church.[5]

---

[3] Wayland, John, *Historic Harrisonburg*, McClure Publishing Company, Staunton, Virginia, 1949, pp. 93-97.

[4] Ibid.

[5] Churchman, Pat, *History of Trinity Presbyterian Church.*

Old Houses in Rockingham County Revisited

RIVER BEND
1833

Prominent among the families following Adam Miller into the county was the Harnsberger family. The first was Stephan Harnsberger, who settled here in 1751. He came from Zurich, Switzerland, settling first in Orange County. Legend tells us that he was a member of Spotswood's exploration party and was the possessor of one of the "Golden Horseshoes."

In 1716, Governor Spotswood left Williamsburg to cross the Blue Ridge Mountains. This was an attempt to encourage settlement in the Western part of Virginia. He had a party of twenty or thirty men with him and for this trip they had a lot of horse shoes with them. Horseshoes were rarely used in the eastern part of the state but were needed for the rougher terrain in the west. Upon their return to Williamsburg, Governor Spotswood presented each of his fellow travelers a gold horse shoe.[1]

---

[1] Wayland, John, *A History of Rockingham County, Virginia*, Ruebush-Elkins Company, Dayton, Virginia, 1912, p.427.

River Bend was built by Jeremiah Harnsberger, the grandson of Stephan. He was married to Elizabeth Miller, a descendant of Adam Miller. (see Adam Miller) Three generations of Harnsbergers lived at River Bend. Jeremiah had a son, Thomas Kennerly, who lived there after his father died. Thomas' son, Charles Graves, lived there until 1908. He left River Bend to go to Harrisonburg and the house remained empty until 1942. At this time Miss Elizabeth Harnsberger, great granddaughter of Jeremiah, took possession. Under her ownership, River Bend underwent a much needed renovation. Upon her death, it was inherited by a family member who then sold it to Merck and Co., Inc. in 1990.

This house is beautifully sited on top of a hill that overlooks the Shenandoah River. It is within two miles of the spot where Governor Spotswood and his Knights of the Golden Horsehoe camped on September 6, 1716. The house is of brick with a limestone foundation. The front door opens into a large center hallway. An open staircase with three landings leads to the second floor and up to the attic. The house originally was a four over four plan but there is now one large room to the left of the center entry hall. The original two fireplaces

Front door and central hallway.

have been replaced with built in book shelves and the fireplace is between them. All the other rooms have a fireplace and mantel.

On the second floor there are four bedrooms with adjoining baths. In the attic, hand hewn exposed "five by five" rafters are evident. A later addition of a porch now covers the area above the original summer kitchen. The basement is accessed from this addition..

The barn was burned by General Sheridan during the Civil War, but the original smoke house and slave quarters stand to the rear of this house. The slave house has two first floor rooms and one large room upstairs.

When Merck bought River Bend in 1990, extensive renovation and restoration was begun. From cellar to attic, Merck has returned this home to its original grandeur. Nearly everything has been restored and it was entirely redecorated in keeping with the period. Merck uses River Bend for entertaining and business meetings. They have taken great pride in this house and it is an excellent example of an important corporate contribution to the history of this area.

MILLER-KITE HOUSE
1827

This house was built in 1827 by Henry Miller, Jr., the grandson of Adam Miller. His name is carved in one of the chimneys. Brick for this house was made nearby and it is laid in Flemish bond. It has four chimneys, two on the east side, one on the west and one on the south. The original house was an ell shape. However, about 1850, a two story addition was built which closed in the ell then making the house rectangular in shape. There are now four rooms on the first floor. There is a single room on either side of the passage in the front. The main stairs is in the front hall. Just before the landing, the stair slides to reveal a hidden compartment. The second floor has four large rooms. The southwest room has a stair case leading to the room below. All the rooms have fireplaces. Over the front door is a fan light with carving.[1] Most of the windows are original and are nine panes over six.

---

[1] United States Government, Works Progress Administration, "Historical American Buildings Survey, Rockingham County, 1935-1939," Bridgewater College microfilm.

Main stairs in the front hall.

Fanlight over the front door.

The frame section extends from the front hall and adds another room. Most of the floors are original heart pine. There are chair rails and wainscoting. All the walls are plastered.

This is an unusual house in that it contains work of a specific craftsman, Samuel Gibbons. He made all the mantels and did all the carpentry and joinery work. His work shows much German influence. An example of this is the tulip and vine motif on the mantels.

This house was inherited by Mary (Polly) Miller, the daughter of Henry Miller. She married John Argenbright. It is known that he operated a tavern during the mid 1850's. It was then passed on to their son, Captain Asher Argenbright. During the Civil War, General T. J. "Stonewall" Jackson used this house as his headquarters April 19-30, 1862 . It is believed General Jackson met with Generals Johnson, Ewell and Ashby here to plan his Shenandoah Valley Campaign. During a one month period of the "Valley Campaign", General Jackson and his troops defeated four Union armies and marched nearly four hundred miles.[2]

---

[2] Douglas, Henry K. 1968, *I Rode With Stonewall*, Chapel Hill, NC, University of North Carolina Press, p.46.

*Tulip and vine
motif on the
mantels.*

Under the front stairway there is a long closet. Written on one of the walls are the initials of some of the soldiers said to have come to the house. The soldiers would probably have been from the 10th Regiment which was made of companies from Rockingham, Page, Madison and Shenandoah Counties.

In 1871, John Cover bought this house and sold it to Captain Hiram A. Kite in 1880. His son was William (Ed) Kite who was Fist Sergeant of Chrisman's Boy Company during the Civil War.[3] (see Contentment) The town of Elkton received this house as a gift from the Kite family in 1984. The Historical Society of Elkton has completed renovations. It is available for tours and for public functions.   VLR; NRHP

William (Ed) Kite

1932 photo taken by John Wayland; courtesy Handley Library, Winchester, VA.

---

[3] Interview with Miss Mary Elizabeth Kite, April, 1999.

MARTIN SPECK HOUSE
1838

This very impressive house was built on the Martin Speck land grant and remained in the Speck family for a hundred years. The original grant consisted of 1100 acres and was the site of two other houses before the present house was built in 1838.

Simply described, it is a house with solid brick exterior and interior walls. It is built on a slight bank with a limestone foundation. The ground floor was where the original kitchen was located and there is a large fireplace for cooking. The first floor is divided into three rooms. It has a center hallway with staircase ascending to the attic. There is one large room to the right of the hallway while to the left is a similar area divided into two rooms. The second floor is identical in layout to the first floor. The house is flanked with four chimneys, two at either end. On the west side these chimneys serve fireplaces in each of the four rooms. The ones on the east side serve only two fireplaces.

In 1937, the house was sold out of the family. The new owners

Photo of the house before the two story columns and second floor balcony were added. Undated photo also shows a family member of the current owners.

then renovated it, retaining most of its original features. A major exterior change was the replacement of the front porch with four two-story columns and a second floor balcony in 1944. It continues to be privately owned by the same family.

BELLE GROVE
1840

It is not possible to trace the ownership of the house because of burnt records. But, Samuel H. Coffman came into ownership of this house in the early 1800's. This house was built by David Coffman, who was a prominent physician before and after the Civil War. It was the scene of much social activity in the county.

When this yellow brick house was built, it was part of an estate which included "Inglewood." Belle Grove is based on the Georgian plan with wide center hall and open stairway. This hall connected to another hall that ran lengthwise with the house. Another stairway here went to the second floor. The rooms were large with high ceilings. There was a fireplace in each room. It has a "L" shaped with a weather board extension giving it a total of sixteen rooms.

Unfortunately, this home is deteriorating badly and is inaccessible by vehicle.

Jennings House
1840

Located in the center of the town of Elkton, this large square brick house built by Dr. Simon B. Jennings in 1840 is an excellent example of more sophisticated architecture in the county before the Civil War. Its design, ornamentation and placement of doors and windows give it a distinctive style from the typical houses built along the Shenandoah River during this period.

It is a two storied house with an almost flat roof. It originally had a " widow's walk". There is a columned porch. The bricks were made in a kiln located on the hill nearby. There are eight rooms, each eighteen feet square. Each room has a fireplace with a mantel. The mantels in the living room and dining room are of dark marble stone. The open staircase is of pine and walnut. It is said that cabinet makers lived in the house while constructing the elaborate wood work.

During the Civil War, this was one of the finest homes in Conrad's Store, now known as Elkton. Conrad's Store was the crossroads to the western gate to Swift Run Gap in the Blue Ridge Mountains. The

Old Houses in Rockingham County Revisited

house was used as a hospital during the Civil War and was later occupied by the Bear, Yancey and Flory families. It was then purchased by the Merck Company and used as a club house. In 1964 it was given by the Merck Company to the town of Elkton. It was first used as the public library. Today it is the town hall and is in excellent condition.

MONTEVIDEO
1840

Albert G. Mauzy (1815-1851) was the son of Colonel Joseph Mauzy and was educated at the Mossy Creek Academy. The Mauzy family was of Huguenot extraction. They first settled in South Carolina and then moved into Virginia. Albert Mauzy became engaged in the mercantile business after finishing school and operated a store at what was know as "Fordwell" on the Shenandoah River. He married Julia Nicolas and moved his store to the west of McGaheysville and called it "Montevideo", meaning 'Mountain View". It is sited at the foot of Peaked Mountain and in full sight of the Blue Ridge Mountains. Other proprietors who operated businesses at "Brick Store" were Sourers, Huffman and Gouchenoer.

The house is a large one, rectangular in shape, built of brick with double porch across the southern side. The building was constructed so that the first floor was utilized as a place of business while the two top floors were used as a residence.

The Mauzys were noted for their hospitality and this house was

Photo taken in 1967 by Isaac L. Terrell showing unpainted brick.

the scene of much social activity as well as being a prosperous mercantile business.

This home has new owners who intend to maintain it as a private residence. It is in good condition.

PEALE HOUSE
CROSSROADS FARM
c.1844

This home is located where the Spotswood Trail crosses the Old Indian Trail. Now a busy intersection, in the 19th century it was the center of much social activity and a prosperous family.

The land where this house stands was originally surveyed to Joseph Rutherford in 1768. It came into the possession of the Peale family in 1811. Jonathan Peale, son of Bernard Peale became the owner in 1831. He is alleged to have built the present house about 1840-1844. While building this house, he lived in a large brick house just west of this one called Hidden Springs. Both houses remained in the family for many years.

The Peale family originated in England, migrating to Pennsylvania and moving from there to the Shenandoah Valley. Jonathan Peale was a justice of the peace and a wealthy farmer. This house is an indication of his desire to impress and to have ample space to entertain. Mrs. Peale offered "Stonewall" Jackson supper and lodging.[1]

This is an imposing house with two story grand porticos porches on

Doric columns on the rear of the house.

the front and in the rear. Six large Doric columns of plastered brick that extend two stories support the two back porches. The brick on the front is laid in a striking variation of Flemish bond. The sides and back are laid in common bond. This house has six thousand square feet.

There are twelve rooms, four on each floor. Each room has a large working fireplace. Nearly everything in this home is original including the windows and floors. Even the interior doors still fit as tightly

Original door hardware.

as they did when the house was built. All the doors have the original locks. There is a large central hall with an elegant staircase. It extends up to one landing and turns to a second landing. Then it splits and rises to both the front and back of the house. There are

[1] John W. Wayland, *Historic Homes of Northern Virginia*, Staunton, Virginia, The McClure Company, Inc., 1937, p.219.

eighteen inch thick brick walls on either side of the hallway to support this staircase.

In 1942, this house was extensively remodeled. All woodwork was refinished. Many of the original mantels were replaced with custom made mantels copied from those in the J. Owen Beard House. There was a spring in the basement which where the original kitchen was located. A dumb waiter originally ran to the basement. Servants were housed in a detached two story building. The original barn still stands and has been renovated into a work space for the owner. There are remains of a grass tennis court that was built in 1875.

This house is privately owned and has been in the same family since 1942. It is in excellent condition.

Undated photo that was probably taken during the Civil War because the men are absent. The ladies are unidentified.

SMITHLAND
1845

Smithland takes its name from Colonel Daniel Smith who was one of the first justices of Rockingham County. It was here that the first session of the court was held in April, 1778. (see Thomas Harrison House) Another house was standing on the place at that time and it is suggested that the first court used this house until a court house could be built. George Washington was entertained twice in that house in 1756 while inspecting forts in the Valley. Colonel Smith died in 1781. His horse threw him during a grand review of the Rockingham Militia to celebrate the victory of Yorktown. In 1842, Daniel Smiths' grandson, Edward Harrison Smith, and his wife, Julia Harrison, came into possession of this property. The present house was built about 1845.[1]

Smithland was built in generous proportions. It has the original

---

[1] Houston Harrison, *Settlers by the Long Grey Trail*, Dayton, Virginia, The Ruebush-Elkins Company, 1935, p.211.

Photo taken in the early 1900's.

tall columned portico and massive brick walls. The foundation is stone.
A wide center hallway is flanked by two rooms on each side. There is
a wide staircase with two landings that rises to the attic. The house
has double chimneys on each end. Each one connects to three fireplaces. Behind the house are the slave quarters which are built of logs
and weather boarded. This is a two story building that accommo-
dated two families per floor. The smoke house has the same roof line
as the main house.

In 1883, Smithland passed from the Smith family to various owners. In 1886, it was purchased by Robert Liskey. The Liskeys did major renovations. Parquet floors covered the original flooring. Bay windows were installed. Beveled glass was placed around the front door.

The Liskeys sold Smithland in 1945 at which time it became a
nursing home. It closed in 1963. Smithland is still owned by the same
family. The current owners have lived there since 1970. Extensive
renovations have been done to restore grandeur to this home. It is in
excellent condition.

George and Ida Liskey relaxing by the front doorway, July 1941.

Below:
Left to Right: Ida Liskey, son Paul, Kate Fleming and an unknown woman. Compare this photo to a similar one of the Peale House.

Bogota
1845

This was the land of Gabriel Jones and his wife, Margaret. Gabriel Jones was born in Williamsburg, Virginia in 1724. His parents immigrated to America from north Wales. He was educated in England and admitted to the bar. He returned to the colonies and settled in what was then Frederick County, now Rockingham.[1] In 1751, he purchased a part of the Jacob Stover tract of 244 acres from Christopher Francisco, whereupon he built his home and occupied it in 1753.

The original home of Gabriel Jones, a one and one half story structure with dormer windows, stood about 100 yards south of the present house. In the autumn of 1784 George Washington visited here and dined with Gabriel Jones. Mr. Jones lived here fifty three years and at the time of his death he owned over 1200 acres of land.

---

[1] In November, 1738, an Act of Assembly passed creating Frederick and Augusta Counties. Until then, the entire Shenandoah Valley was made up of Orange County, In 1777, a large part of Augusta County was cut off to form Rockingham County.

Unknown person holding painting of the original home of Gabriel Jones. Photo taken in 1932 by the Historic American building Survey; courtesy of the Library of Virginia, Richmond, Virginia.

He was the first "King's Attorney" to become a resident of Augusta County and represented the county in the House of Burgesses in 1757, 1758, and 1771. In 1788 he was a member of the Virginia Constitutional Convention.

The present house was built about 1845 by Jacob Strayer, Jr., formerly of New Market who purchased the land in 1831 and lived in the old Gabriel Jones house while he was building the brick house.

It is now a spacious, English style house, two stories high and "L" shaped, containing twelve rooms. There is a wide center hall with open staircase ascending to the attic. All rooms have fireplaces and mantels. The exterior is ornamented with a two storied two-column portico with balcony, It is said that during the battle of Port Republic members of the Strayer family sat on this balcony and watched the movement of the battle on the plains beyond the river.

The house and farm have remained in the hands of the same family. Bogota has been maintained in excellent condition.

Photo of Bogota taken in 1932 by the Historic American Building Survey; courtesy of the Library of Virginia, Richmond, Virginia.

Old Houses in Rockingham County Revisited

HIGGINS HOUSE
1848

When this brick house was built, it was part of a five acre tract conveyed by Reuben Harrison to Jeremiah Kyle (see Homeland) in 1824. It was deeded to Dr. Henry R. Higgins in 1848 and it was he who built the house.

It is an "L" shaped house. A two story kitchen structure was separate. Originally there was a twelve foot walkway where food had to be brought to the south facade of the ell. It is believed that the kitchen was connected soon after construction. A pair of end chimneys are on the main block. Two other chimneys are on the "L".

The front door has a triangular pediment with transom and sidelights, typical of the Federal period. The lintels above the windows are simple. Many of the windows are original. They are twelve over twelve panes high. During the Civil War, signatures of residents were etched on a pane. There was a bay window added later to the north facade of the house but it was removed when the street was widened. The central hall is flanked by two symmetrical rooms. However, the rooms on the south side have more decorative woodwork, indicating they might have been used for entertaining. A doorway in the front left room leads to the rooms of the ell. The dining room was probably the main room downstairs because there is a built in cabinet. A door at the end of the dining room leads to the kitchen. The second floor is identical to the first floor. The left front room here has access to the rooms in the ell.

This house has an enclosed porch which was added later. It runs the length of the ell and the rooms in the ell open onto the porch. There are two steps down because there was originally a smaller porch here. The foundation is cut limestone.

Isaac Hardesty, who was the first elected mayor of Harrisonburg, lived here in 1849. He was a merchant and political figure. While he was mayor, the town prospered in the years before the Civil War. He established Rockingham Savings Bank, which was the first of its kind in the area. Previously, the closest banking center was in Richmond.

The most recent occupant of this house was a business. It is now unoccupied.

Isaac Wenger House
c.1848

This large brick house is built on a slight bluff overlooking Linville Creek.. It was built on land owned by Samuel Coffman, whose home "Mannheim" is located on the opposite side of the creek.

The land here was a part of a survey granted to Joseph Kratzer (see Kratzer House) and Jacob Custer in 1784 and was purchased by Samuel Coffman in 1830. In 1851, it was divided by his sons. One of them was Isaac Coffman, who is thought to have built the house some years previously. In 1863, it was purchased by Isaac Wenger who was reputed to have owned about 1700 acres of land including two large flour mills.

The house contains twelve rooms. There are six chimneys which serve thirteen fireplaces. There is one in each room and one in the basement. This house is an indication of the prosperity existing in the county during this pre-Civil War period. It was built in an "L" shape with wide center hall and open staircase, ascending to the attic.

Hook and claw iron bars.

The front portion contains eight rooms while the rear extension contains four. Unusually large for this period, this house has iron hook and claw braces that run through the floorboard to the exterior walls. The brick was made on the premises and painted. An unusual feature is the dinner bell on top which has a cord that runs down to the kitchen. One of the largest barns in the county stands on this property. There is a detached building that was a private residence at various times.

The house and farm remained in the Wenger family until 1912, when it was sold out of the family. One family has owned this house since 1916. The house has recently been sold. It remains in excellent condition as a private residence and is undergoing renovations.

Dinner bell.

SOLOMON FUNK HOUSE
1859

This limestone house was built by Solomon Funk in 1859. Solomon Funk (1825-1880) was the thirteenth child of Joseph Funk (see Joseph Funk House). He was married to Elizabeth Koiner from Waynesboro. While the sons of Joseph Funk were originally of the Mennonite faith, they became affiliated with the Baptist congregation of Turleytown. Solomon Funk became a minister and missionary. For many years he preached throughout the county. He was the postmaster of Singers Glen as well as a printer, farmer and like the rest of his family, a lover of music. Many members of the Funk family are still active in the community.

Although this house was built later than the time scope of this survey, it is so distinctive in style that it deserves attention. Most stone houses built in the county have pitched roofs and end chimneys. This house is almost square. The chimneys are enclosed and it has a hipped roof. While it appears to be a two storied house, it is actually three. The first floor is partially below ground, opening on the ground level on the west and south sides of the house. The kitchen and dining room are on this level. The second floor above the kitchen level has a center hallway with a room on either side of the hall which runs the depth of the house. The open stair case ascends to the attic. There are three rooms on the third floor. Interior walls are plastered. The six column, Greek Revival portico at each end of the house is gone but the pediment roofs have been saved and are in storage. The exterior limestone walls are still in excellent condition.

This house has been unoccupied for many years. Once inside, despite the deteriorating conditions, evidence of fine workmanship is seen in the woodwork. The mantels are plain as well are the door and window trim. The floors are original. The interior doors have been painted with grain decorations on the hall side, but remain undecorated from the inside. Another decorative feature that can still be seen is the painted decorations on the risers of the stairs in the center hall. The current owners intend to renovate this once beautiful home.

Mason House
1875

While this house was not built during the period covered in this volume, it is architecturally significant and warrants being included. Outstanding among the stone houses in the county, it is almost square in shape with an extension to the south side. It has a flat roof which is not typical of stone houses in this area. It also shows a distinctive if not artistic handling of a natural material.

The house was built in 1875 by Robert J Mason who was a stone mason and stands as a monument to his skill, the likes of which is not to be seen in any other house in the county. Mr. Mason built the house for himself and quarried the stone from nearby. On the east side, between the two front doors is a piece of stone, twelve inches wide and reaches from porch floor to the ceiling. It is carved to represent a pine tree. Near the top is the stone builder's signature, R. J. Mason, and the date 1875.

Back row: Robert J. Mason and his wife Mary Magdalene Shank Mason. There were two other children who died.

Below: This photo shows Robert J. Mason and his family on the front porch of the Mason House. The boy sitting on the fence in front of the house is Charles Kendrick who was raised by the Mason family.

Mr. Masons' granddaughter was able to provide some information about Mr. Mason and his experience in the Civil War. He wrote a letter to his daughter about this war experience. He was opposed to the war, therefore he did not volunteer immediately. Finally, he was drafted after the Battle Of Manassas. After serving in the Winchester area, he traded with a man to become a bugler. He was chief of ambulance operation in the Siege of Petersburg. He also served as guard for President Davis. He says he was in the war for three and one half years and did not fire a shot at the Federals. A family story indicates that he left without being mustered out. He then was afraid he would be accused of desertion. He hid for awhile in the hills near the location of this house. He was a farmer and carpenter. He died in 1926 at the age of 85.

The house itself is plain and depends upon the quality of the cut stone for its type. The stones are laid linearly and with design rather than at random as the other stone houses in the county. They are cut long, the largest stone measuring five feet in length and twelve inches high. An interesting feature of the stone, besides the smoothness of the cut, is the combination of the gray and yellow color. The yellow in the limestone is caused by the clay seepage into the rock seams and whether this was by design or developed as the stone weathered is speculative. By contrast to the superior dressage of the stone on the front and sides the back of the house is less carefully laid, not unusual in the construction of county houses.

Originally there were nine rooms in the house, but now there are seven as a result of the partitioning of rooms. The interior woodwork is solid walnut including the rafters. The kitchen originally was in the basement. Outside there is a spring that is never dry.

The house is in excellent condition. There present owners have lived there since 1972.

GLOSSARY

Baluster—an upright support for a railing

Balustrade—a series of balusters with a rail

Bank House—a house that is built into the side of a slope so that there are two ground floor entrances

Batten—strips of wood on the top and bottom of a door.

Common Bond—a bond in brick laying consisting of four to six bricks between a single header

Corbel—a bracket or block projecting from the face of a wall that supports a beam

Cornice—a projecting section along the top of a wall that is decorative

Dependency—a structure serving a main building-smokehouse, loom house

Dormer—a vertically set window on a sloping roof

Doric—Classical Greek style that shows heavy fluted columns without a base

Dovetail—a projection at the end of a piece of wood that can be put into a corresponding opening at the end of another piece to form a joint

Eaves—a projecting overhang at the lower edge of a roof

Ell—an extension of a building at right angles

Fanlight—a semicircular or fan-shaped window with radiating members set over a door

Flemish Bond—a bond in brick laying in which each row consists of alternate headers and stretchers with the headers centered on the stretchers of the row below and above

Fluted—having regularly spaced vertical, concave and parallel grooves as seen on a column or pilaster

Gable—a triangular section of the wall underneath a double pitched roof

Graining—painting on a surface to imitate stone or wood

Header—a brick laid with the length across the thickness of the wall

Hipped Roof—a roof with four uniformly pitched sides

Keeping Room—sitting room

Lean-To—a simple addition that has a single pitched roof set against a larger building.

Lintel—a horizontal piece over a door or window

Mortise—a hole cut in one piece of wood to receive a tenon

Pediment—a triangular crowning element used over doors

Pilaster—a shallow attachment of wood to a wall to resemble a column

Portico—a major porch with a pediment roof supported by columns

Reeding—parallel convex molding; the opposite of fluting

Scroll work—decoratve work cut of thin wood with a narrow saw into curved pieces

Step ends—decorative scroll work on the side of a staircase

Stretchers—bricks laid out the length of the wall

Stucco—rough plaster often laid over brick

Tenon—end piece of a piece of wood to fit into a hole or mortise to make a joint

Tongue and Groove—a joint made by fitting a projecting strip along the edge of one board into a groove cut along the edge of another board

Wainscot—wall paneling of wood

Weatherboard—cover and protect a surface with a thin board thicker on one edge than the other edge; clapboard

Old Houses in Rockingham County Revisited

INDEX

Old Houses in Rockingham County Revisited